BIBLE READING NOTES

mettle

TO INSPIRE COURAGE SPIRIT CHARACTER

MIX
Paper from
responsible sources
FSC® C013417

Copyright © YFC and CWR 2013

Published 2013 by CWR, Waverley Abbey House, Waverley Lane, Farnham,
Surrey GU9 8EP, England. Registered Charity No. 294387.
Registered Limited Company No. 1990308.

Mettle Bible-reading notes are produced in association with British
Youth for Christ. British Youth for Christ is part of Youth for Christ
International, a movement of youth evangelism organisations in over 100
countries of the world. Please visit www.yfci.org for the country nearest you.

Series Editor: Simeon Whiting
Contributors: Chris Kidd, Hannah Kidd, Phil Knox, Judy Lloyd,
Paul Stockley, Simeon Whiting

The notes on 'Mission and Evangelism' were previously published in *Mettle*
Jan–Apr 2010.

See back of book for list of National Distributors.

Unless otherwise indicated, all Scripture references are from the Holy Bible,
New Living Translations (NLT), copyright © 1996, revised 2004. Used by
permission of Tyndale House Publishers, Inc., Wheaton, Illinois 60189. All
rights reserved.

Other quotations are marked: NIV: Scripture quotations taken from The
Holy Bible, New International Version (Anglicised edition), copyright ©
1979, 1984, 2011 by Biblica (formerly International Bible Society). Used by
permission of Hodder & Stoughton Publishers, an Hachette UK company.
All rights reserved. 'NIV' is a registered trademark of Biblica (formerly
International Bible Society). UK trademark number 1448790.
NCV: Scripture taken from the New Century Version, copyright © 2005
by Thomas Nelson, Inc. Used by permission. All rights reserved.

Concept development by YFC and CWR.

Editing, design and production by CWR.

Printed in Wales by Stevens & George Print Group.

CONTENTS

WELCOME TO **mettle**

COURAGE SPIRIT CHARACTER ...

I WONDER WHAT IMAGES come into your head when you hear the word 'Missionary'. In our core readings, we'll think about how we can be missionaries and evangelists without even leaving home!

We've also got some tasty hot potatoes lined up. A lot of people say they don't care about politics, until a politician does something they don't like! Let's talk about how we can engage with politics in a godly way. Then, we'll move on and reflect on Ethics and Integrity. How can we live well for God? And just in case it's all sounding a bit dry and intellectual so far, we'll go for the heart to finish. We'll explore emotions: anger, depression and happiness in particular. We'll look at some examples of Jesus' own emotions and think about how He can help us manage ours.

Enjoy!
The *Mettle* Team

MISSION
+ EVANGELISM

IF YOU HAVE STUDIED *Romeo and Juliet* at school you will know that someone's last words are really important. As he is dying, Mercutio declares: 'a plague o' both your houses' – and it means bad news for all involved. Jesus' last words to His disciples, however, are even more important and are about good news. After rising again from the dead, He tells all who follow Him to spread the good news about a God who loves individuals enough to die for them and who wants a relationship with them.

The word Christians use for this spreading of good news is 'evangelism', a word that is understood in all kinds of ways: from the preacher with a sandwich board on the street corner, to the American guy on television passionately asking for donations. When Jesus told

'Therefore, go and make disciples of all the nations ...'

people to 'go and make disciples' I'm not convinced these are the kinds of things He expected us to be doing.

However, He did want us to lead people to follow Him by our actions and our words – making disciples is something for all of us to do. It is one of our purposes as Christians. It is not always easy but it is one of the most exciting things we can do.

Over the next couple of weeks we are going to look at 'Mission and Evangelism' and find out how we can change the world by leading others to follow Jesus. This week we are asking why we share our faith and next week we'll think about how we go about it. The first reason for telling others, as we read in today's passage, is because Jesus tells us to. As Christians we are to take God at His word and do as He says.

WED 1 MAY

5

↑ PRAY

Father, please speak to me over the next couple of weeks and help me to understand more about why and how I can tell others about You. Amen.

'... Christ's love controls us. Since we believe that Christ died for all ...'

KEY VERSE v14

THURS 2 MAY

6

THINK

Which people would you love to see come to know Jesus? Pray for opportunities to share God's love with them.

When we think about why we tell other people about God, it's helpful to think first why God sent Jesus to show us the way to Him. Jesus said: '... God loved the world so much that he gave his one and only Son ...' (John 3:16). We tell other people about God's love for them because we love them. We want them also to know the truth – the way to real life on earth and life forever in heaven.

Imagine you were wandering in a desert, incredibly thirsty, when you found a spring of drinking water. If you then bumped into other people in the desert, you wouldn't keep that news to yourself, would you? You wouldn't want them to go thirsty; you would tell them, in order to save them. So, by telling others the good news, we show that we want to see them saved; that is, accepting the love of a Father who gave His Son as a way to receive forgiveness.

In today's passage Paul says that Jesus' love controls us – a better translation is 'urges us on'. In other words, God has placed His love in our hearts which then spurs us on to tell other people about Him. Later it says, 'God has given us this task of reconciling people to him' (v.18). We share His love that has been shown to us, by telling others about it.

KEY VERSE v26

'Then Jesus told her, "I AM the Messiah!"'

This week we have looked at the fact that we evangelise because Jesus tells us to, out of our love for people and because it's such good news and is worth telling people about. We finish this week by looking at an encounter between Jesus and a woman whose life is changed through meeting Him. Therefore, another reason for evangelism is that it has the potential to totally transform people's lives: the impact of them becoming Christians is massive.

Have you ever received some good news that changed your life? I remember when I received a phone call telling me I'd got the job I really wanted; and when I got good exam results; and when my little brother was born. Each time my life was changed in an amazing way. I just wanted to tell everyone!

We see the same in this passage. When the woman finds out that Jesus is the Messiah her life is totally changed – but it doesn't end there. She then goes and tells everyone about it. So, what's stopping you? Find the courage to tell your friends today.

FRI 3 MAY

7

PRAY

Father, help me to understand why it is so important that other people come to know You. Help me to be available to be used by You to tell others and to show them the way to You. Help me to love my friends the way You do. Amen.

KEY VERSE v39

'Many Samaritans from the village believed in Jesus because the woman had said, "He told me everything I ever did!"'

Last week we looked at *why* we evangelise and this week we will be looking at *how*. We start where we left off yesterday, with the woman whom Jesus meets at the well. Her life is transformed through an encounter with Him and then, in our passage today, the story continues. This woman courageously goes and tells her whole village about Jesus. The people believe and are totally changed themselves.

So what special words does the woman use? The woman simply tells her story of how meeting Jesus has impacted her life. We too can tell our story of how Jesus has impacted our lives.

Sometimes we hear the amazing stories of gangsters or drug dealers. They used to do loads of awful stuff, then they met Jesus and everything changed in an incredible way. When we hear these stories it can be very tempting to believe that our story is not really

that interesting; that it would not make a difference to anyone else. We feel that our personal story isn't as powerful as those of other people.

If you are a Christian, God has changed your life – and that is a story worth telling. Whether it's the story of how you became a Christian, how your life has changed or just a moment when you knew that God was real, your story could have a huge impact on a friend's life. The great thing about your story is that no one can argue with it. People can criticise your faith, but if you say, 'This is something that happened to me', there is no way that they can disprove it.

What happens when the woman tells her story? Many Samaritans from her village believed in Jesus (v.39). Today, know that your story has power and pray that many come to know Jesus through you.

CHALLENGE

Think about your story. How has God changed your life? Now go and tell your story to at least one person today.

'I bring you good news that will bring great joy to all people.'

KEY VERSE v10

THINK

What is the best piece of news you have heard recently? What did you do with it? What do you feel is good about following Jesus? How can you tell your friends this?

Evangelism is often called 'preaching the gospel'. The word gospel means good news. We tell other people about Jesus because He tells us to, because we love people and because it is such good news that we shouldn't keep it to ourselves.

I am very romantic – so much so I got engaged in a muddy car park! However, when my girlfriend said 'Yes!' I was so happy that I phoned all my family and friends and texted my whole phone book. I wanted to stand on top of a building and shout my news at the top of my voice.

The good news about Jesus is not just good news; it is the best news in the whole world. What a story! That the King of kings and Creator of the universe loved the world so much that He became a baby, who grew into a man, who died on a cross to restore the way for a relationship with Him and real life on earth and forever!

This is the news that the angel brought to those shepherds as Jesus was born, and it's the kind of news that we should want to share with everyone. God's love is all about good news.

KEY VERSE v3

'Pray for us, too, that God will give us many opportunities ...'

Billy Graham is one of the world's most famous evangelists. He has told over two billion people about Jesus; so he must know a thing or two about evangelism! A friend of mine asked him, in connection with telling people about Jesus, what the three most important things are. He replied: 'Prayer, prayer and prayer.' Praying for our friends is so important when we want to see them become Christians.

It is said that another evangelist, D.L. Moody, prayed for one hundred of his friends to become Christians. Before he died, 97 of them became Christians. The final three accepted Jesus at Moody's funeral – awesome!

In this passage Paul urges us to devote ourselves to prayer, watching what is going on and being thankful. Pray for your friends!

Pray also for opportunities to share your story, to serve people or to talk about your faith, as Paul prays (v.3). I remember reading this when I was about fifteen, and praying, 'Please, Lord, give me an opportunity to share my faith today' – and having three or four chances before lunch time. What a dangerous prayer!

TUES 7 MAY

11

CHALLENGE

Today, make a list of ten of your friends, like D.L. Moody did, and start to pray for them. Put the list in your Bible and commit to praying for them for as long as it takes. Be patient – and keep going.

'But you will receive power when the Holy Spirit comes upon you. And you will be my witnesses ... everywhere ...'

WED 8 MAY

12

PRAY

Lord, help me to talk more openly about You and to have the confidence that You are with me during tough times of questioning. Amen.

Jesus had died, risen from the dead and was about to go back up to heaven. Before this event takes place He tells His disciples that the Holy Spirit will come and give them power to tell others about Him. This is one of the purposes of the Spirit – to give people power to tell others about Jesus. In this account retold by Luke in Acts, Jesus then goes back to heaven. The disciples are still scared, but then, days later, the Holy Spirit arrives.

Peter changes from someone afraid even to leave the house to a man who stands up in front of a massive crowd and tells them all about Jesus. That day about 3,000 people decide to follow Jesus. (Read about it in Acts 2:1–41.)

I remember one night while I was leading a weekend away with my youth group. A few of them who weren't Christians started asking lots of tough questions about God. I didn't really have the words to say or the confidence to say them, so I prayed: 'God, would You help me?' The next thing I knew, I was explaining really difficult things with words and ideas that I never normally would have had! It was as though the Holy Spirit was helping me to find the right words. You too could pray that the Holy Spirit would come and help you.

KEY VERSE v16

'In the same way, let your good deeds shine out for all to see, so that everyone will praise your heavenly Father.'

Jesus was not just somebody who talked a good game. He taught amazing truths that changed people's lives and He led them to God. He also lived a life that made a difference and showed people the right way to live. In this passage He calls us to do the same.

Jesus says that we are 'the salt of the earth' (v.13). What does salt do? Salt has healing properties and can be used to preserve food and keep it fresh – like olives in a jar. And, if it's all over your chips, you know about it because it makes a difference – it is distinctive. So, Jesus asks us to lead lives that make a positive difference; lives that stand out. If we just blend in and follow what the rest of the world does, we are good for nothing.

He then says we are 'the light of the world' (v.14). What does light do? It is attractive and shows people the way. So also we are to love people and show through our attitudes that we have a relationship with God, being grateful and joyful.

Then imagine what could happen! In the passage, Jesus says that people will praise God (v.16). In other words, the people we touch may become Christians themselves!

THURS 9 MAY

13

Is your lifestyle drawing people to Jesus? Are you salty and distinctive enough? Think about what else you could do to be like salt and light in the world.

THINK

'And if someone asks about your Christian hope, always be ready to explain it.'

KEY VERSE
v15

CHALLENGE

Inviting our friends to a special event is a brilliant opportunity we can take to help us share the gospel. This may be an event at church, a carol service, an Alpha course etc. If you don't find it easy to speak, then get others to help you to take the first steps.

People often quote St Francis of Assisi as saying: 'Preach the gospel at all times and, if necessary, use words.' What he was saying is that we can evangelise just by the way we lead our lives – and we only need to use words if we have to. I agree with him that it's important to live in a way that attracts people to Jesus, but I believe we should also use words to tell people about Him.

Jesus demonstrated this by the amount of speaking He did – both to the crowds and to His friends. Peter says that we should always be ready to give an answer to anyone who asks us to explain our hope in Jesus. I think that telling our story is a massive part of this but we also need to know God's Word (the Bible) and give answers to questions our friends might ask.

Think today about what you would say if someone asked you why you are a Christian. Ask yourself: What are the main questions my friends are currently asking? If you struggle with knowing the answers, ask a youth leader or pastor to help you. Be ready to speak words that may change your friends' lives.

'Now [Christ] is far above any ruler or authority or power or leader or anything else – not only in this world but also in the world to come.'

KEY VERSE V21

POLITICS

THE WORD 'POLITICS' is not found in the pages of Scripture. However that does not mean there is nothing about politics in the Bible. On the contrary it has at least as much to say about politics as any other ancient manuscript or religious text.

So what is politics? Just as when we talk about economics we are essentially talking about money (or wealth and resources which have some monetary value), so in a similar manner, when we talk about politics we are essentially talking about power. Particularly, we are talking of government and other public institutions of authority.

CONTINUED ▶

In the world that we live in, power may be held by a few people over many others, either with or without their consent. However in Scripture there are many narratives about people in power (in the historical books), and critiques of their use of this power (in the books of the prophets), and principles to guide those in power (in the wisdom literature).

So instead of looking for the word 'politics', if we search for words such as 'power', 'authority', 'rule' (and 'ruler'), 'govern' (and 'government'), 'prince', 'king' etc we will get a much deeper and clearer insight into a godly perspective on politics.

PRAY

Paul prays that his readers would come to understand that as followers of Jesus they are called into an inheritance that is beyond anything any government can offer. Christ has ultimate power. Ask God for insight as you learn what the Bible has to say about politics.

KEY VERSE v21

'But select from all the people some capable, honest men who fear God and hate bribes. Appoint them as leaders ...'

Even great leaders can get things wrong. Moses was a great leader. But leadership should not be about status – a person holding the exalted title of 'leader'. Leadership should be about function – a person's capability to do the task of leading. It is no good being called a leader if you can't lead! And Moses was now failing in this.

He had been faithfully fulfilling his God-given role since the people fled captivity in Egypt. However, in his diligence Moses was exhausting himself. He felt the weight of responsibility for resolving the people's disputes, providing consistent governance. But, he was not coping with the heavy workload, and in his busyness he lacked the creativity to see that there were other ways of solving the problem.

Step in Jethro. His sage advice helps to develop a new basis for governing the nomadic nation, sharing the responsibility among a number of appointed skilled leaders, each representing a constituency of the people. These two principles (people's representatives, shared leadership) are key to more responsible and accountable styles of government today, just as in Moses' day.

MON 13 MAY

17

PRAY

Thank God for your politicians, who work to represent their constituency (you and your neighbourhood) in parliament. Ask God to give politicians diligence and humility as they share in the task of government.

"'Do everything they say to you," the LORD replied, "for it is me they are rejecting, not you. They don't want me to be their king any longer."'

KEY VERSE
v7

PRAY

Whatever the political system, we should pray for those in power to govern wisely for the benefit of the people. Do so now!

During the Arab Spring from 2010 through 2011 and 2012, in many nations (Egypt, Libya, Yemen, Tunisia, and more) people have risen up to bring down corrupt rulers and force change in the political system. Some protests have brought a violent response from those in power, leading towards civil war. Other changes have been more peaceful. In the past, many European nations have also seen revolutions, some long and violent (eg France, 1789 to 1799), others short and peaceful (eg Czechoslovakia, 1989).

Today, when we see problems in the political system, it is tempting to say: 'Politics does us no good,' or, 'We need a new system that is fairer.'

In the days of Samuel, the Israelites felt like that. For many years they had been led by judges – some good (like Deborah), some awful (like Abimelek). But in this passage we see that now, they want to change the political system. They want a monarchy instead. Fortunately, it was not a violent revolution, but God warns them that changing the political system will not solve their problems. Any power structure can be corrupted, because the problem is human sin and rebellion against God.

'When Haman saw that Mordecai would not bow down or show him respect, he was filled with rage.'

WED 15 MAY

19

What happens in the corridors of power? Usually we don't see what is going on behind the scenes. We just hear the media reports and the politicians' sound bites, or in some cases the spin doctors trying to put a bad policy decision in a positive light. But whatever they say in front of the cameras, it can be quite another matter behind closed doors.

Have you noticed how when things go wrong in government, nobody will take the blame, but when things go right, everybody claims the glory? See how that approach works out in today's reading. Here we have a failed assassination plot. But notice that it is not the whistleblower who gets applauded. Mordecai gets completely overlooked by the king while Haman takes the glory. So, Mordecai refuses to salute Haman, but Haman plans a scheme to shift the balance of power even more in his own favour.

CHALLENGE

Dig out a newspaper today. It shouldn't take you long to find some examples of a politician passing the blame, or taking the glory. Pray for integrity for your political leaders.

'Queen Esther replied, "If I have found favor with the king ... I ask that my life and the lives of my people will be spared."'

KEY VERSE v3

THINK

Read through today's passage again. As you do so ask yourself: is this justice or is it revenge? What do you think?

'How come they seem to get away with it?' Do you ever think like that? Rogue politicians and greedy bankers rarely seem to end up in court, and certainly not in prison! Nicking one item from a shop gets five years in jail, but a city dealer may gamble away millions worth of other people's hard earned savings and walk away. You get a long sentence for stabbing someone, but start an illegal war that results in the deaths of 10,000 innocent civilians, and it may be that you simply smile, shake hands and retire on your government pension.

Sometimes, the tables are turned. And of course, we all celebrate such sweet vengeance. 'Justice is done,' we assert. But revenge and justice are not the same thing. Revenge wants 'pay back', often out of malice, whereas true justice seeks to penalise wrongdoing and restore order to society.

In the story of Esther there are many political twists and turns, plots and sub-plots. In today's reading Haman's scheming plans backfire. Outwitted by Mordecai and Esther, he falls from power, losing his life.

'Meanwhile, the other Jews throughout the king's provinces had gathered together to defend their lives ... killing 75,000 of those who hated them.'

The book of Esther ends with a brutal massacre, not of the Jewish people, but of their enemies. Interestingly, it does not seem to be enough for the Jews to just defend themselves. The passage states that they take two days to kill off anyone with whom they have a disagreement, and then conclude with a big party to celebrate their victory.

Notably, God is not mentioned in the whole book of Esther. Some scholars imagine that God's invisible hand is at work in the background. But it does seem a bit strange not to give God credit if this be the case. Other scholars say that God is silent because He is not involved and does not approve. While things turn out in their favour, Esther and Mordecai both have significant character flaws. So perhaps this is just a story of political intrigue ...?

Sometimes politicians with religious affiliations are too quick to claim that God is on their side, despite their evident failings. The truth is, God is not 'on the side' of any one party or other. The real question is whether political leaders honour God in how they perform their role as servants of the people. Do you think they do?

FRI 17 MAY

21

CHALLENGE

The story of Esther is not a long one. It is worth reading the whole book. As you do so, ask yourself: would God approve or not? Do the leaders show integrity?

KEY VERSE
v10

'Feed the hungry, and help those in trouble. Then your light will shine out from the darkness, and the darkness around you will be as bright as noon.'

Have you ever seen a homeless person sleeping in a street doorway? Ever heard of an elderly person left without medical care? Ever felt the pain of a young person struggling with a learning difficulty and excluded from school or given up for foster care? Of course you have, probably several times. Maybe even among your own family and friends.

What's this got to do with politicians fiddling their expenses, or the meltdown in the banking system? How is

this affected by government policy on corporate taxation, or employment legislation, or the state of the economy?

According to Isaiah, the answer is, quite a lot! It is all a question of priority. There's a saying in sport, 'don't take your eye off the ball'. When you cease to focus on what is most important, then everything else begins to fall apart too. And Isaiah says society's primary focus should be on the most vulnerable people. If this is made a number one priority, then society as a whole will flourish.

CHALLENGE

The next time you stumble across a homeless person in a doorway, why not buy them a sandwich and a cup of tea? Choose to be part of the solution, not part of the problem.

'God gave these four young men an unusual aptitude for understanding every aspect of literature and wisdom.'

KEY VERSE
v17

THINK

How can we live in a worldly culture without living by worldly values? How far is it possible, do you think?

In the year 605 BC Nebuchadnezzar, the king of Babylon, invades Judah and abducts the sons of Judah's elite leaders. The king intends to indoctrinate them to serve in the Babylonian political system. Here we have the story of four of these teenagers.

They are surrounded by a pagan culture that does not acknowledge the one true God, or the moral standards of their faith. Instead, people here worship many false idols and human ideals. The teenagers even have their names changed, and are named after pagan gods. As part of their physical and mental training, they have to learn the language and literature of this pagan culture. But they are also expected to change their ways and customs, including eating food and drinking wine which has been sacrificed to pagan gods. Now the question is: are they going to compromise their faith, or are their actions going to give honour to the one true God?

You also are surrounded by a worldly culture that often does not acknowledge God and has moral values that are in conflict with your faith. It is OK to learn about the world around you, but be careful about being influenced by worldly values, which often do not honour God.

KEY VERSE
v6

'Anyone who refuses to obey will immediately be thrown into a blazing furnace.'

Unlike Judah's monarchy, Babylon had quite a complex political power structure. In the UK there is The House of Commons: elected politicians, including The Cabinet (the inner circle of ministers with special areas of responsibility), and The House of Lords: unelected overseers who review government decisions and laws. There is also a separate judiciary with judges and magistrates. What system of government is there in your country? We don't know all the details of Babylon's government, but how many different roles can you find in verse 2?

Some political leaders get drunk on power. Instead of remembering that they are given power to serve the people, they imagine that everyone is there to serve them, and they lust after more power to boost their own egos. You do not have to look far in the history of any political system (ancient or modern) to see people like this. See if you can think of some examples!

Nebuchadnezzar was one such leader. In Daniel 2:47 he acknowledges the one true God, but by chapter 3 he has forgotten all about Him, and demands everyone's allegiance to worship a new idol.

TUES 21 MAY

25

THINK

Imagine you were one of the four teenagers we read about in chapter 1. What options do you think are open to you? What would you choose to do? We will read the rest of the story tomorrow!

'But even if [God] doesn't [save us], we want to make it clear to you, Your Majesty, that we will never serve your gods ...'

KEY VERSE v18

WED 22 MAY

26

Now we see the outcome of yesterday's scenario. Sometimes people under oppressive tyrants choose to simply obey, even though it may go against their conscience. Sometimes they find ways to resist, which may be violent or non-violent. Daniel's friends choose non-violent resistance, simply refusing to compromise, and end up in jail and then sentenced to a terrible execution in a furnace. They are confident that God could rescue them, but even if this does not happen, they are determined to do what they believe is the right thing.

Many people who stand up to abuses of power don't know what the outcome of their actions will be. Of course they hope it will bring about change for good, but they may be jailed (or even executed) and forgotten about.

It is easy for us reading the story. But if you didn't know what the outcome would be, would you still do what was right in this situation?

PRAY

Pray for people who are imprisoned for their religious or political convictions. Ask God to give them the courage to do what is right, even though this may cost them their lives.*

*If you want to find out more and help people who are imprisoned unjustly, check out www.amnesty.org.uk. For organisations that support the international Persecuted Church look up www.barnabasfund.org or www.opendoorsuk.org.

'For seven periods of time, let him have the mind of a wild animal instead of the mind of a human.'

Do you ever have weird dreams or nightmares? When you wake up, you wonder, 'What was all that about?' In today's reading we have a weird dream of an enormous tree reaching into the stratosphere, visible from the horizon, with lush leaves and fruit feeding every creature on the planet, it seems. Next thing it is felled and the stump is bound up with strong metal cladding, still rooted in the dirt.

What's that got to do with politics? In the Bible we have this strange kind of literature called 'apocalyptic', which comes out in visions and dreams, mainly in the books of Ezekiel, Daniel and Revelation. It uses picture language of bizarre plants and creatures, and also superhero figures, something like a Marvel comic. It is often about world powers and empires rising up and being overthrown in the course of human history. And about the ultimate sovereignty of God's kingdom.

Although King Nebuchadnezzar has acknowledged God's power, he has not confessed his own arrogance and seems unwilling to humble himself before God. And now he is having nightmares, and wondering if he is going insane! Actually, he is!

THURS 23 MAY

27

Read the 'comic book style' passage again and ask yourself: what warnings are there here for today's political leaders?

THINK

'King Nebuchadnezzar, please accept my advice. Stop sinning and do what is right. Break from your wicked past and be merciful to the poor.'

KEY VERSE
v27

FRI 24 MAY

28

CHALLENGE

Do you know who your local MP is? If not, find out! Do you know what they think about issues which affect you? When is the last time you asked God to guide their policy decisions? Do so now!

There are different ways of engaging with any political system. Unlike in chapter 3, where Daniel's friends simply oppose the king and refuse to obey his orders (because they go against God's law), in chapter 4 Daniel takes a different approach. This time he uses his influence to explain to the king the consequences of his actions, and to try and persuade the king to change his ways. He gives some fairly strident advice (v.27)!

We can also engage with our government and politicians in different ways. As political activists we can go on protest marches to oppose unjust laws and abuses of power. These often get into the news headlines. But it is worth considering what you are trying to achieve. Are you trying to get publicity for a cause? To embarrass the government? Or to bring about real change? Sometimes there is a place for this type of action and other acts of 'civil disobedience'. But on other occasions the smart thing to do is to go and meet personally with our political leaders and explain our concerns, and why we think the government should alter its policy.

'... this is what he requires of you: to do what is right, to love mercy, and to walk humbly with your God.'

ETHICS +INTEGRITY

ETHICS AND INTEGRITY are complex issues, but hugely important too. Integrity (or lack of it) can make a dramatic difference to every decision we make and change the whole course of our lives. In the next fortnight we will look at the insight various parts of the Bible give us into integrity and ethical living. We will learn from the experiences of a range of biblical figures and allow God to challenge and inspire us to show integrity in our own lives.

Today we start with a crucial principle from the Old Testament. Apparently there was once a man who wanted to know how often the Bible spoke about poverty and justice. He cut out every reference he could find and spread them over his desk. What surprised him the most was how little was left of his Bible – only

CONTINUED ▸

odd pages here and there. In total he found over 6,000 passages that he needed to read. Many of them came from the Old Testament.

The Old Testament contains a detailed ethical code. In this, moral problems such as adultery, war, punishment, parent-child relations, the use of property and the treatment of the vulnerable are all addressed. The prophets often helped to interpret the Ten Commandments and the wider law for their society. In the same way as we experience today, the written law often needed to be interpreted and applied and the prophets were crucial in this.

The overarching theme in today's reading is to do the right thing and to love mercy. This is a common theme throughout the ethics of the Old Testament and something that is no less relevant to us today.

PRAY

Father God, I pray that you would help me to follow the command of Micah in today's key verse, to 'do what is right' and 'to love mercy'. Amen.

'But I warn you – unless your righteousness is better than ... the teachers of religious law ... you will never enter the kingdom of Heaven.'

We started this series on Ethics and Integrity by looking at a central ethical theme of the Old Testament. Over the next few days we turn to what we can learn about God's idea of ethical living from the Gospels.

In the book of Matthew, the Sermon on the Mount is key. This is where Jesus outlines His guidance for ethical living. He calls for a life of complete devotion to God, a raising of the bar from the Jewish standards.

Today's key verse shows us that Jesus called for a radical kind of righteousness that outstripped the way the Jewish teachers of religious law had done things previously. He wanted His followers to embrace His way and to be distinct in their attitudes and actions. And the same applies to us today. The Sermon on the Mount highlights the fact that living life as God wants us to will often involve behaving differently from other people. Living the way God commands will be distinctive and will make us stand out. It may be costly but it is crucial if we are to honour Him.

MON 27 MAY

31

CHALLENGE

Take the time to read through the whole of the Sermon on the Mount (Matthew chapters 5–7) and to be challenged by Jesus as to the way we should live our lives.

'... If any of you wants to be my follower, you must turn from your selfish ways, take up your cross, and follow me.'

KEY VERSE
v34

THINK

Spend some time reflecting on how you would answer Jesus' question about who He is. What might it mean for you to take up your cross?

Today's Bible reading contains the famous question asked by Jesus: 'But who do you say I am?' (v.29). Our response to this question should shape the way in which we live our lives.

If you were to answer Jesus' question, you might do so in many ways which contain truth. Jesus was a miracle worker – able to heal people, turn water into wine and walk on water, amongst numerous other miracles. He was also the Son of God, the promised Messiah. But Jesus wants to draw our attention to the fact that His purpose was to suffer and be killed. He goes on to tell us that if we want to follow Him, we must also take up *our* cross. To follow Jesus with integrity means to be willing to lay down our lives.

Living life in the way God wants us to is not going to be easy. Yesterday we discovered that living by His standards is not the same as living by the general standards of the world. It is more than that, and as a consequence it will often be hard. But if Jesus is Lord of our lives then we must follow His example, take up our cross and be willing to suffer in His name.

KEY VERSE
v25

'... you had everything you w
Lazarus had nothing. So no
being comforted, and you are in anguish.'

In the book of Luke, caring for the marginalised in society is a key theme. For example, Luke is the only Gospel that documents the visit of the shepherds, who were near the bottom of the social ladder, when Jesus was born.

In Luke 4 Jesus quotes from Isaiah and in doing so sets a vision for His ministry, rather like a presidential speech or the launch of a new *Apple* product. He talks about how He has been sent 'to bring Good News to the poor ... to proclaim that captives will be released, that the blind will see, that the oppressed will be set free' (Luke 4:18).

In today's reading, we hear about a rich man, and a poor man named Lazarus. If you look at the story carefully, you will see that there is no suggestion that the rich man was ever unkind or nasty to Lazarus; he simply ignored him. Jesus shows us that ignoring those in need around us is not living the life that God intended us to live.

CHALLENGE

Reflect on who is marginalised in your community and in the wider world. Who would Jesus go out of His way to spend time with? How could you show God's love and care for these people?

'Your love for one another will prove to the world that you are my disciples.'

KEY VERSE v35

In John's Gospel we find very little by way of explicit moral or ethical teaching. However, we can gain some understanding of how God wants us to live from two key themes evident in the book of John: life and love. Throughout John's Gospel we read how Jesus has come to bring life. For example, He talks about being 'the way, the truth, and the life,' (John 14:6), 'the bread of life,' (John 6:35) and being the good shepherd who gives his sheep 'eternal life' (John 10:28). As well as Jesus telling us that He came to give life, He also demonstrates it through many miracles involving healing people and raising the dead.

For Jesus, loving people and bringing them life go hand in hand. He demonstrates His love for the disciples by washing their feet. In this act of service, He serves them humbly. His command is that in our lives we should be willing to put our own needs aside to love and care for others and enrich their lives.

CHALLENGE

Who has God put around you? Which people do you encounter every day? How could you love them and enrich their lives?

KEY VERSE v5

'You must have the same attitude that Christ Jesus had.'

Paul generally writes to individuals and communities of Christians who he knows well and who look to him for guidance and advice. Often in his letters he attempts to guide them through some of the difficult issues that have arisen in their different situations. So his letters are full of insight and godly advice into real, complex, ethical issues. For example, should a new Christian divorce their unbelieving husband or wife? How closely should a Christian be involved with non-believing friends and pagan practices?

Some of the specific issues that Paul addresses will not be directly applicable to us and our own situations. However, we can still learn from the instructions that he gives to the Christians he writes to and the general principles behind those instructions. In today's key verse, Paul tells us that we should have the same attitude as Jesus. In the verses around this we learn a bit more about what he means by this. Paul calls believers to put their own wants and desires aside and follow Jesus' model of love and self-sacrifice.

FRI 31 MAY

35

THINK

Think of an ethical dilemma you're facing at the moment. How would an attitude of love and self-sacrifice change your response?

KEY VERSE
v23

'Hypocrites! ... you ignore the more important aspects of the law – justice, mercy, and faith.'

WEEKEND 1/2 JUN

36

Are there some rules that you find it easier to stick to than others? Perhaps ones that fit conveniently with your everyday lifestyle, or those that make you look good in front of other people? The Pharisees were like that, concerned with what made them look holy and religious. They attempted to lead a morally correct and blameless life but missed what was really important. They were so concerned with following the letter of the Jewish law that they overlooked the values of justice, mercy and faith which were at the heart of the law. They failed to act ethically and with integrity because they'd lost touch with God's heart and what He sees as important.

When thinking how best to live a life of integrity, we

need to look to Jesus first and foremost. If we try to keep the commandments given by God throughout the Bible, we will go a long way towards living the life He intended, but as we see from the Pharisees, this is not a sure-fire way to ensure we do the right thing. We can still miss the heart behind these commandments. The key to living God's way is not a written commandment but a Person. Jesus Himself modelled a righteous, godly life. To live a life of integrity, we should follow the One who told us, 'I did not come to abolish the law of Moses or the writings of the prophets. No, I came to accomplish their purpose' (Matt. 5:17).

PRAY

If you're facing any kind of ethical dilemma, commit it to Jesus now. Ask Him to remind you of what's really important and to give you wisdom to respond to this situation in a godly way.

'The woman was convinced ... So she took some of the fruit and ate it.'

KEY VERSE v6

MON 3 JUN

38

THINK

In what ways are you tempted to go against the will of God and the instructions He has given for living? How could you respond wisely to peer pressure or other things trying to pull you in the wrong direction?

Sometimes knowing what we should do can be a tricky business. We're not always entirely sure what to do for the best. However, at other times we can know exactly what we should do and still find it hard to do it.

In today's reading, Eve knew exactly the way in which God wanted her to behave. She knew that she should not eat the fruit the serpent showed her. However, the serpent talked her into eating it and she broke the rules by which she was meant to live.

We can find all sorts of excuses to go against what we know is right. Perhaps all our friends are doing it, perhaps we think we'll be better off as a result of doing it, or perhaps we justify it by saying it won't do anybody any harm. But God gives us rules to live by in order to make sure we live the full life that He intended for us. By going against His will, we will compromise our ability to live the life He intended for us and miss out on the blessings that it brings.

KEY VERSE v2

'Take your son ... Go and sacrifice him as a burnt offering on one of the mountains, which I will show you.'

Ever done something absolutely crazy? I can remember watching four of my friends do a bungee jump and thinking they were totally out of their minds! Sometimes God might ask us to do something which looks crazy to other people. In today's passage we read how He commanded Abraham to sacrifice his son. If you know much about the story of Abraham then you will remember that he and his wife Sarah had longed for children and this was their firstborn child. Imagine you were a friend or servant of Abraham's. Watching him go to sacrifice Isaac you would have thought he had gone mad. But Abraham trusted God and was prepared to do what God asked him to do – even when it seemed mad.

Following God's guidance for our lives won't always make sense to people around us. They might think we are strange or simply wrong for doing what we do and thinking what we think. It is not necessarily the easy option. It might even go against what we have previously told ourselves is the right thing. But we need to be in tune with God's views and be prepared to follow Him even when it seems to go against our better judgement.*

[*Be careful with this though! God will never ask us to do something which harms ourselves or other people.]

TUES 4 JUN

39

CHALLENGE

In what areas do you find it hard to go along with God's thinking? Talk to a trusted older Christian about this, pray about it, then take a deep breath and obey God!

'Don't ask me to leave you and turn back. Wherever you go, I will go; wherever you live, I will live.'

KEY VERSE v16

PRAY

Thank You, Father, that You see the bigger picture of our lives. Help us to be like Ruth and to trust in Your guidance and leading even when others believe we should go a different route. Amen.

In the time when these events took place, it would have been customary for wives whose husbands had died to return to their families unless there was another relative from their husband's family who could marry them. This was the situation that Ruth and Orpah found themselves in, so their mother-in-law, Naomi, tells them to go back to their families. Returning to their family was the normal and expected course of action, but Ruth decides to go against tradition and stay with Naomi.

Ruth's action is a classic example of going above and beyond the call of duty. Nobody would have thought any less of her for leaving Naomi and heading for home, but Ruth was not prepared to do that. She felt such a sense of loyalty to Naomi that leaving her seemed out of the question, even though this was a far easier option.

Sometimes God may call us to do something that doesn't seem to be in our best interests. Others may tell us we're crazy and encourage us to take an easier option, but are we confident enough in God's guidance to go against the advice of others who see our situation from a worldly point of view?

KEY VERSE v33

'Have I tried to hide my sins like other people do, concealing my guilt in my heart?'

Most people could list a whole load of ways in which they have lived good lives. They might say they've helped other people or given money to charity or simply that they haven't murdered anybody or stolen too much! In this chapter, Job is protesting that he has lived righteously. He defends himself from the suggestion that he's guilty of some kind of sin by going through a whole list of expectations for what a righteous life might look like.

This list can be quite a challenge as we read it. Can we, like Job, say that we have never looked with lust at a member of the opposite sex (v.1)? Or that we've never lied to someone (v.5) or acted unfairly (v.13)?

Today's key verse is a particularly hard-hitting challenge. Job recognises that many people try to hide it when they have done something wrong. They think that so long as nobody knows, then nobody will come to any harm. Often the sins that people struggle with are secret sins. Nobody knows about them and so we find it difficult to deal with these things. If there's something we're struggling with in secret, it is definitely a good idea to talk to someone we trust. This person can pray with us and help us to overcome our struggles in Jesus' name.

THURS 6 JUN

41

THINK

Is there a sin you're trying to hide in your heart? Who could you turn to for help?

'Joseph ... was a good man and did not want to disgrace her publicly, so he decided to break the engagement quietly.'

KEY VERSE v19

FRI 7 JUN

42

What would happen if a friend of yours was cheated on by their boyfriend or girlfriend? I'm sure if it happened to one of my friends, everybody would know about it. Rumours would spread and other people would think badly of the person who had been unfaithful.

Picture the situation with Mary and Joseph. They were due to get married but then Joseph finds out that Mary is pregnant. Of course the only logical possibility is that she has slept with another man. Joseph must feel betrayed, humiliated and extremely angry.

When we feel strong emotions like Joseph would have done, it can be difficult to act with integrity. But Joseph managed to respond with grace and dignity. He didn't want to humiliate Mary and leave her open to the danger of being executed. Instead he decided to discreetly break off the engagement. As well as this, he continued to be open to God speaking to him in the midst of this difficult time. Because of this, he heard what God said, listened to Him and went on to marry Mary.

PRAY

How do you think you would have reacted in Joseph's situation? Spend some time asking God to help you act with integrity when crises hit your own life.

'So God created human beings in his own image. In the image of God he created them; male and female he created them.'

EMOTIONS

WEEKEND 8/9 JUN

I'M BAD AT BEING EMOTIONAL. Or, more to the point, I'm bad at understanding what I'm feeling and why. There are times when this is useful. It means I can stay calm and make rational decisions when people around me are getting angry or upset. But it can be a real weakness too. It also means when I'm upset I tend to bottle things up and only express what I'm feeling when it all gets too much – regardless of whether or not that's a good time to do it! And in the meantime, I find myself getting angry over really insignificant things and not knowing why. I sometimes feel sorry for the people who have to live with me!

However well we handle our emotions, let's recognise they're an important part of what it means to be human.

43

CONTINUED ▶▶

God created each of us to look like Him in terms of our ability to think, but also our ability to feel. If we ignore our feelings, or try to repress them (as I tend to), it means denying a crucial part of who we are, and how God has made us. On the other hand, that doesn't mean we should always act on our feelings. For example, our capacity to get angry is God-given, but that doesn't mean we're always justified in being angry and certainly isn't a licence to hit anyone who winds us up.

This series of readings is all about the feelings we experience and how we can handle them in a godly way. We'll also reflect on examples of God's emotions which we find in the Bible, and what we can learn from them.

PRAY

Lord God, thank You for creating me with emotions. Please help me to handle and express them wisely. Amen.

KEY VERSE v2

'We were filled with laughter, and we sang for joy.'

What makes you laugh? For reasons far too complicated to explain here, my brother and I burst out laughing every time we hear the town of Barnsley mentioned! We may find different things funny, but each of us has a sense of humour and all of us like to laugh. I think this is God-given. God created us with emotions, because He wanted us to be like Him and emotions are a part of who He is. But I think God also gave us emotions because He wanted us to enjoy life. I believe that He wants us to laugh and enjoy the good things that life brings us.

Living God's way should be a joyful thing. That's not to say it'll always be easy (more on that tomorrow), but following God certainly shouldn't be boring. It should be a challenge, an adventure filled with God's joy. In today's passage the people of Israel weren't afraid to express their joy at being back in Jerusalem after years of exile. They may have wept whilst they were exiled but they didn't forget to rejoice when it was all over either. As we do our best to live God's way, let's be open to the joy He gives us and not afraid to laugh and express our emotions.

MON 10 JUN

45

THINK

How are you using your God-given sense of humour? Do you take life too seriously? Is your type of humour appropriate for a Christian? (See the Humour series in the Jan–Apr issue for more on this.)

'Though you do not see him now, you trust him; and you rejoice with a glorious, inexpressible joy.'

KEY VERSE v8

TUES 11 JUN

46

I have a friend who always seems to be smiling. Partly, that's an element of his personality, but you can also see God at work in him through it. His life certainly hasn't been easy. He's been through plenty of tough times, including losing his dad at a young age. But whatever life throws at him, my friend always seems full of God's joy.

The fact is that life is hard. Of course we won't always be happy. It can be a real struggle to keep going with God and keep trusting Him, especially when we can't see Him and we're trying to deal with huge problems. But in the midst of trouble, we can still have a deep sense of God's joy. The challenge here is that joy is often a choice. Whatever is going on around us, we can choose to rejoice, worship God for who He is and praise Him for all the good things He has given us.

CHALLENGE

However happy you're feeling right now, choose to rejoice! Remember who God is and the good things that He's given you. Praise Him and thank Him for those things.

KEY VERSE v23

'Guard your heart above all else, for it determines the course of your life.'

This verse shows us just how powerful emotions can be. If we respond emotionally to things we see, hear and experience, without thinking about them, they can affect us deeply and even change the whole direction our lives may take. This is particularly true of romantic relationships. You probably know people who seem to fall in love easily. They rush from one relationship to another, following their feelings, apparently without thinking about whether this new relationship is really a good idea. Sadly this attitude can lead to them being deeply hurt and damaged by people who perhaps didn't really care for them in the first place.

It applies to other areas of our lives too, though. For example, if we're over-sensitive when criticised and take to heart every comment people make about us, we can easily feel hurt and maybe even end up angry and bitter. Emotions are healthy and natural, but unless we couple them with a healthy dose of wisdom, it's all too easy to get hurt. Emotions are powerful things. Let's not forget this.

WED 12 JUN

47

CHALLENGE

Choose to 'guard your heart' by thinking about the people you allow to influence you. Weigh up comments people make about you before you take them to heart. And don't rush into any close relationships just because you're following your feelings.

'Each heart knows its own bitterness, and no one else can fully share its joy.'

KEY VERSE v10

THURS 13 JUN

48

Probably one of my greatest flaws is how reluctant I am to talk about how I'm feeling. As long as I'm happy, everything's fine, but when things start to go wrong, I find myself trying to deal with a lot of fear, frustration and anger – on my own. It might seem obvious to you, but it came as a bit of a revelation to me that I actually felt much better once I started opening up to my friends and telling them how things really were.

It's probably true that no one else can completely understand what you're feeling, but they'll get a much clearer idea if you talk to them about it. Perhaps it comes naturally to you to tell your friends what you're going through and how you're feeling. Perhaps you're more like me and this takes a bit more effort. However easy it does or doesn't feel, it's definitely worth the effort. Don't struggle along on your own and don't isolate yourself from people who might be able to help you. On the other hand, don't keep quiet when things are going great either! Share your joy with the people around you.

PRAY

Thank God for the good friends He has given you. Ask Him to prompt you to share your feelings with them and to support them when they're struggling too.

KEY VERSE v17

'With his love, he will calm all your fears. He will rejoice over you with joyful songs.'

I love the idea of God singing. It's a striking and unusual image. Unfortunately, far too many people think of God as being angry, rather than anything else. There are things which make God angry, as we'll see tomorrow, but this is just one small part of His character. The Bible gives us examples of God showing all kinds of different emotions. Today's reading, for example, shows God singing – expressing deep joy.

The fact that God expresses His joy in this way should encourage us to openly express our joy when we feel it, too. We may not be great singers, but expressing our joy lets other people share in it. And the reason why God is singing should encourage us too. He sings because He's so delighted with His people – and that includes you and me! It isn't conditional on anything we do or say; God rejoices over us with joyful songs, purely because He loves us. Maybe that should get us singing too!

FRI 14 JUN

49

THINK

How do you react to this picture of God expressing His joy? How does it affect your own attitude towards expressing your emotions?

KEY VERSE
v8

'So put on clothes of mourning and weep with broken hearts, for the fierce anger of the LORD is still upon us.'

WEEKEND 15/16 JUN

50

We might not like to talk about it, but unfortunately there's no getting away from the fact that there are things which make God angry. In these verses, we see a very powerful – almost shocking – description of God's anger. The reason God is so angry is that the people of Israel and Judah have turned their backs on Him. They know very well how He has provided for them and protected them in the past, but they have chosen to ignore Him and worship other gods instead.

The people go through the motions of worshipping God, thinking that just saying or singing the right words will be enough, but their hearts aren't in it. They're not interested in what God really wants from them and can't be bothered to obey His commands. They worship God in the Temple but forget about Him as soon as they walk out of the door. And, as we read on in Jeremiah, we find that God's people are cheating one another and exploiting the poor, while making themselves richer.

All this should make us stop and think. God takes this kind of thing seriously. He won't punish us in the same way He punished Israel and Judah (see Rom. 8:1–2), but if we ignore Him and exploit other people, it makes Him angry. So is there anything we need to change about the way we treat others and our attitude towards God?

CHALLENGE

Ask God to show you if there's anything wrong in your treatment of others or your attitude towards Him. Be open to God revealing one or two things which you need to change. Then, have the courage to change those things.

'How often I have wanted to gather your children together as a hen protects her chicks beneath her wings, but you wouldn't let me.'

KEY VERSE
v37

MON 17 JUN

52

THINK

Jesus' heart breaks when the people He loves suffer but won't have anything to do with Him. How can we help people who are suffering see how much Jesus loves them?

There's nothing worse than seeing someone you love suffer. When my son was a year old, he developed an illness called croup, which made it very hard for him to breathe. The illness got so severe that he ended up in hospital, in intensive care. It's difficult to describe how awful it felt to watch my son suffering and be completely unable to help him. He eventually recovered, but I've never forgotten that feeling.

Jesus expresses a similar feeling here. He can see the people are harassed and helpless, struggling through life and oppressed by the religious teachers. He desperately wants to help them, heal them and restore their relationship with God, but they're not interested. He sees them suffering, He certainly could help them, but they won't let Him. Quite simply, this breaks Jesus' heart.

This should both inspire us and challenge us. It should inspire us to rely on God when we're suffering. He loves us and wants to help us and comfort us in the hard times. It should also challenge us to share Jesus' love with the people around us, particularly when they're suffering.

KEY VERSE
v33

'... a deep anger welled up within him, and he was deeply troubled.'

We've mentioned anger a couple of times in this series already. But this is a different type of anger. This is anger mixed with deep sadness and grief. This is compassion. In this passage, Jesus sees the people around Him grieving for Lazarus – particularly Mary and Martha whom He knew very well – and He's overcome with sadness because of it. The really remarkable thing about this is that Jesus must have known what He was going to do next (see vv.23–26), but He is still profoundly moved by this situation, even to the point of tears (v.35). I find it hugely comforting to know that when I'm suffering, Jesus feels my pain deeply, yet still has the power to transform the situation.

Compassion isn't just about feeling sad when someone else does. It means doing something about it. In Jesus' case, He did the most incredible thing possible in these circumstances – He raised Lazarus from the dead. When we're moved by an awful situation, how ready are we to show Jesus' brand of compassion and get involved to change things?

TUES 18 JUN

PRAY

If you're suffering, thank Jesus that He's with you, feels your pain and can transform the situation that you're facing. If you're doing fine, ask Him to help you have His compassion for others and to act to change painful and difficult circumstances.

'... Jesus entered the Temple and began to drive out the people buying and selling animals for sacrifices.'

KEY VERSE
v15

WED 19 JUN

54

Ever get angry at something silly? I'm generally quite laid back, but a sure way to get me angry is to come between me and my food! It's amazing how easily we can get angry over things which don't really matter. In the incident we've just read about, Jesus is obviously very angry. It would be easy for us to use the fact that Jesus got angry as an excuse for our own anger, but that's missing the point.

Here, Jesus got angry because poor people were being exploited. The individuals selling animals for sacrifice would have conned poor people by telling them the animals they'd brought to sacrifice weren't good enough and charging them far too much to buy different ones. Not only were the poor being ripped off, but the stall-holders were making it unnecessarily hard for them to worship God. Jesus was furious and went so far as to call these sellers 'thieves' (v.17).

There is a time and a place for righteous anger like this. It means being so close to God that the things which make Him angry make us angry too. This is the kind of anger which motivates us to take action against injustice in God's name.

PRAY

Ask God to reveal His righteous anger about things which are wrong and unjust and help you to express it. (Be careful that you don't just use this as an excuse for getting angry about something silly!) Then take action to help change these things.

KEY VERSE
v44

'... he was in such agony of spirit that his sweat fell to the ground like great drops of blood.'

Stress can affect us in a variety of ways. Apart from the mental and emotional effects – inability to concentrate, sleeplessness, loss of appetite, anger, anxiety, depression – stress has clear effects on the human body too. Increased heart rate, nausea and aches and pains are all common physical symptoms of stress. But in the most extreme cases, it has been known for the sufferer to actually sweat blood. This is known as hematidrosis.

The fact that Jesus sweats blood at this point is an indication of the extreme stress and fear He is experiencing. Well aware of His impending death, He wrestles with the enormity of it all as He prays. Jesus was completely God but at the same time completely human. He experienced every temptation we experience and every emotion imaginable, from happiness to the extreme fear and stress that we see in today's reading. There is nothing, absolutely nothing, we can go through which Jesus doesn't understand.

THURS 20 JUN

55

Whatever you're going through right now, Jesus is with you and understands what you're experiencing. How does that affect how you feel about the situation?

THINK

READING: Matthew 9:35-38

'When he saw the crowds, he had compassion on them because they were confused and helpless ...'

KEY VERSE
v36

FRI 21 JUN

56

About a year before I wrote this, the UK was rocked by a week of violence as people took to the streets, rioting, destroying property and looting shops. The news was full of shock and speculation about why people would do this kind of thing. At its heart, I think the problem was that the rioters were like sheep without a shepherd: they had nobody to guide them and direct them into something more positive. (The government's report into the riots tells us that poor parenting and a lack of positive role models were significant causes.)

When people have no clear guidance or direction, they can end up doing all sorts of things which damage themselves and other people. Jesus notices this lack of direction in the crowds around Him and He feels deep compassion for them. But Jesus doesn't stop at just feeling sorry for the people. As we've seen already in previous days' readings, He takes action, healing them and telling them what it means to know God. Then He turns to the disciples and challenges them to get involved too. For all these confused and helpless people to hear the good news, far more people are needed to heal them and teach them, as Jesus did. Could that include you and me?

CHALLENGE

Pray that God will send out more people to spread His message of good news through words and actions. Be open to the possibility that you might be one of those He sends!

'... [Jesus] called his twelve disciples together and began sending them out two by two ...'

KEY VERSE
V7

MISSION
+EVANGELISM

WEEKEND 22/23 JUN

IN MAY, WE LOOKED at why we share the good news of Jesus and also how we can share it with our friends and those around us. Now we will take time to look at where we can go with this news. We'll also see whether we can learn some lessons from a great evangelist who was fearless in his obedience to Jesus.

Have you ever thrown a stone into the water and seen the ripples spread wider and wider into huge circles? Even if the stone is small, the ripples can affect an enormous area of water. When we look at how fast the good news of Jesus spread, it's incredible to think that not only did the gospel spread out from the land of Jesus' birth to other countries, but it carried on spreading until it reached you and me in our own country in the twenty-first century. How amazing to realise that

CONTINUED ▶

we are included in God's great plan of evangelism and mission – whoever we are and wherever we live.

The word mission comes from the Latin word *missio* which indicates the sending out or releasing of someone to keep spreading the good news. So, over the next two weeks, we will be looking at how this happened and how we can be involved in the continuation of this exciting mission! Each one of us has a part to play in the big picture of evangelism and mission.

Today's Bible reading shows us that Jesus started with the 12 disciples. He sent them out with His authority and power. At this point in history, I'm sure that this small group of guys had absolutely no idea of how big the plan really was!

PRAY

Father, thank You so much that Your good news has arrived to change my life. Please help me to see how I can be part of Your unstoppable mission over the coming weeks, months and years. Amen.

'Then [Jesus] said to the disciples, "Anyone who accepts your message is also accepting me."'

We have seen that Jesus' mission started with just twelve disciples. Today we look at the next team that Jesus sent out: six times bigger than the twelve. Even before they set out, Jesus said that the work was so huge that they should be praying for more people to join the team!

Have you ever spent time with a leader who thinks big? He or she is very likely to give you something to do which makes you think: 'I can't do that!' But then you try it – and succeed. Then you find out that your leader has even bigger things for you to do.

When Jesus sends anyone out on mission, it can be scary – but those who step out and obey often end up feeling full of joy and surprise. That's how the 72 disciples came back. So what's the secret behind all this? It comes down to five important words from Jesus – '... go ... I am sending you ...' (v.3). When you know Jesus sends you on mission to tell others about Him, wherever that is, you have all the authority of God behind those words.

MON 24 JUN

59

THINK

Have you ever had a sense of God sending you out on mission? Are there ways in which you can do this, either with your youth group, church or a youth organisation you know?

'... I will pour out my Spirit upon all people. Your sons and daughters will prophesy.'

KEY VERSE
V17

TUES 25 JUN

PRAY

Father, I pray that You would fill me with Your Holy Spirit so that I can have the courage to carry on Your mission. Amen.

Today we read about a spectacular example of Jesus' mission. The strange thing is that Jesus was no longer here on earth as a man. A recipe for disaster ... or maybe not!

Have you ever been given a big job to do when the person who asked you to do it has disappeared somewhere, leaving you feeling very alone? It can be a test of courage to keep going.

In today's reading, we learn about what happened when Jews from all over the world, in Jerusalem at the time, saw 12 guys stand up together to make a very important announcement. One man, with a very loud voice, delivered a message from God – and the result was that thousands of people became followers of the one Person who wasn't there ... their leader. Or was He there after all?

The mission was bigger and faster after Jesus finished His part of the work and returned to heaven. His Holy Spirit was given to every one of His followers to carry on the mission. That means us too – so let's get involved!

KEY VERSE
v4

'But the believers who were scattered preached the Good News about Jesus wherever they went.'

Most of the evangelism and mission that we have read about so far has been to one group of people – the Jews. But things were moving fast and another path opened up ... leading to a very undesirable group of people.

How do we feel when we see groups of people who do things or dress differently from us? Or, what about when we are with someone who makes us feel very negative? We can often find ourselves taking sides – or just mixing with a select group of people we feel comfortable with. It would be very hard to be told to go and give this gift of good news to people so different from us.

But taking God's gift of good news meant breaking down lots of prejudice, starting with a group of people Jews despised – the Samaritans. Today's reading shows how Philip smashed through this barrier by following Jesus' example and preaching to the Samaritans. This was the start of many barrier-smashing missions which would eventually bring the gospel to us today.

PRAY

Lord, help me include everyone in Your mission, just as You have included me. Please forgive me if I have thought that some people should be excluded from hearing Your good news. Amen.

'So beginning with this same Scripture, Philip told him the Good News about Jesus.'

KEY VERSE v35

THINK

If God made this meeting happen, He can bring people into your life so you can help them. Get ready and read your Bible as much as possible – it's the source of wisdom!

Sometimes we meet someone 'by accident' and, looking back, we realise that it wasn't a random meeting at all. I can remember someone coming to talk to our youth group about the need for Christian teachers in the Comoro Islands, and six months later I was flying out to an island in the Indian Ocean to join a Christian missionary group there. It was no accident that I was asking God what He wanted me to do that very day when the speaker turned up!

The reading today shows that God cared about someone on a desert road, who was trying to read a book he didn't understand. So He sent Philip to explain everything to this VIP. The Ethiopian became a follower of Jesus and carried the good news home to North Africa.

God intends His message of good news to spread to all places on the earth; to have an impact on the lives of those who hear His Word. We may not all be called to take the good news to Ethiopia, but we are all called to spread His good news wherever we are.

If we get involved in mission, who knows whose path we will cross!

KEY VERSE v34

'... Peter replied, "I see very clearly that God shows no favoritism."'

We can get impatient when people repeat things to us, especially if we heard the first time around. But when God says the same thing three times, we know we are either hard of hearing or we need to change something major in our lives. It must be extremely important news! When was the last time someone said exactly the same thing to you three times – or even twice? It's usually because they want to make sure you heard the important news.

Peter's big lesson from God was that the gospel was for all – including the occupying force of the land: the Romans. No wonder the message had to be repeated three times, because it was against the Jewish law to mix with these people (v.28). But through Peter's obedience, the door was now wide open for everyone in the world to hear the good news.

Jews, Samaritans, Africans and now all Gentiles (non-Jews) are included through a specific message from God Himself. God was teaching His servants that there are NO exclusions for the mission of Jesus. Every country, every people group and every individual from here to the ends of the earth can be included in God's kingdom (see Rev. 5:9).

FRI 28 JUN

63

CHALLENGE

How big is your vision for spreading the gospel? Do you have any ideas or barriers in your mind that may need changing? Ask God to help you to overcome these barriers.

KEY VERSE
v15

'... the Lord said, "Go ... Saul is my chosen instrument to take my message to the Gentiles and ... to the people of Israel."'

Last week, we looked at how the good news of Jesus spread out from Jerusalem. Starting with a few disciples, the good news spread into a worldwide missionary Church with thousands of believers.

Now we will look at one person who experienced a dramatic turnaround in his life. This man, who tried to live his life as an example for others, can teach us so many lessons about mission. Leadership in Jesus' eyes isn't always the same as the leadership we see around us. So we need to be prepared for a few surprises along the way as we look at the life of a man named Saul, later to be called Paul.

In today's reading, we see the power of Jesus at work in Saul's life. Within about 72 hours, a man filled with extreme hatred for Jesus, who persecuted believers, was transformed: he became one of the greatest missionaries of all time. How amazing is God! Saul suddenly realised that Jesus had died for him too and he couldn't keep this news to himself. He devoted his life to the work of spreading the good news of Jesus. Through him, many learned what it was to take the good news to other people.

What about you? Jesus may have already called you to follow Him, but what about the second part? Do you know that there is mission work to do and there are lots of things Jesus wants you to do with His help? It may be that, like Ananias, you can share the good news in your own town. Imagine if one person was to come to know God through you – that would be amazing! As you read about Paul this week, make time to pray and listen out for God's mission plan for you.

PRAY

Father, thank You that I have work to do for You. Please speak to me this week as clearly as You spoke to Paul and Ananias. And help me to obey You when I do hear Your voice. Amen.

'... the Holy Spirit said, "Dedicate Barnabas and Saul for the special work to which I have called them."'

KEY VERSE v2

MON 1 JUL

66

Teamwork is very important. I've been part of many teams involved in mission work, both here at home and abroad. When I was in the Comoro Islands, we all had different jobs to do: teaching, nursing and administration. However, we all had one common aim: to make the love of Jesus known to people who didn't know about Him.

Think about a team you are in. Could you actually get the job done well if you were on your own? Jesus had many plans for Saul but he was sent out with other people so they could help each other. Even the 12 disciples who we read about last week were sent out in twos ... no loners!

So let others help you in mission. Let people pray for you, advise you, support you financially and send you out! Be bold in asking for people's support – if God is calling you, He will give you what you need. And we can start here in our own area before going further afield.

I am involved in sending young people out on overseas mission, and there is always a team of people at home who help with the preparation before the volunteers join a team in another country. You are part of a big worldwide family – so don't go on mission alone, wherever you find yourself.

CHALLENGE

Have you ever allowed people to pray for you, encourage you and send you out on mission, here or abroad? There are wise people around you. Listen to their wisdom.

'I have made you a light to the Gentiles,
to bring salvation to the farthest
corners of the earth.'

In today's reading, Paul was over 400
kilometres away from home. He couldn't
just jump on a plane or hire a car, either!
The travelling was hard, long and very tiring,
but there was a driving force in Paul that
kept him going through thousands of miles
of travel and heat.

Not only was the journey long, but the
reception committee at the other end wasn't
exactly friendly, once the Jewish leaders
heard the message! It's always interesting
to see what happens to people when things
don't go to plan ... Paul and Barnabas faced
jealousy, arguments, insults – and then
violence erupted.

What do we do in these circumstances?
Take courage, remember God's calling on your
life and keep going! Paul was even bolder. He
said he would preach to the Gentiles and went
on to the next location on his tour.

When Paul and Barnabas left, it was up to
others to take the good news and it spread
through the whole area. Once God starts
something, no one can stop it!

TUES 2 JUL

67

THINK

Facing difficulties and opposition can be part of mission. Are there opportunities right now where you can stretch your faith and be bold in Jesus' name?

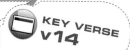

'... the Lord opened [Lydia's] heart, and she accepted what Paul was saying.'

KEY VERSE v14

PRAY

Father, help me to be obedient to You; to keep on sharing Your good news and to leave the results to You. Amen.

What does it take to get your full attention? What happens when you're listening to someone talking and you hear your phone ringing or a text message arriving? Do you really listen to anyone – or are you easily distracted?

In today's reading we see that the Lord had to quieten Lydia's mind and heart so that she could concentrate on Paul's message, but it took an earthquake to make the jailer sit up and listen to him (vv.26–27)! The end result was the same: both wanted to know more about Jesus, but the circumstances in which they were saved were different.

When you get involved in taking Jesus' words to people, different things will happen. We need to be confident that we're in partnership with God – so expect the unexpected! It won't take much to make some people understand the love of Jesus, whereas it might take a whole lot of shaking to make others listen. The one thing Paul and Silas did was to keep going – through the good times at the riverside and the bad times in prison.

So what should we learn from today? We have our part to play and so does God. So keep sharing the good news wherever you go, keep praying, praising and obeying God – and let Him do the rest.

'... [God] commands everyone everywhere to repent of their sins and turn to him.'

When God sends you out on mission, there will be things you see that start to trouble you. This is often a good thing because it makes you want to get up and do something about it!

In today's reading, Paul was very troubled when he saw all the idols everywhere in Athens. So he had a good walk around and then saw a way of speaking to the people about the God who created everything. Have a look and see how he introduces the God they didn't know about!

God can open our eyes to what is going on in the world, at whatever age we are! I met one family who took their children to Zambia and Botswana in Africa – one boy was eleven and the other was eight. The older boy was so moved by what he saw that he told his parents he wanted to train as an electrician and go back to help the people. The younger one was upset by the needs he saw. He learned that the children may not have had many material things, but they had family and community which were very strong and supportive.

Paul was also in a place away from home where there was a great need to make Jesus known. His concern about this prompted him to take action.

THURS 4 JUL

69

THINK

God may want you to step out of your comfort zone and see places where there is a lot of spiritual and physical need. Do you need to explore some options? The needs may be within your own community.

Why not listen to Kelly Greene's story on:
www.24-7shorts.com/prayer-as-justice

'Keep putting into practice all you learned ... from me ... Then the God of peace will be with you.'

KEY VERSE v9

FRI 5 JUL

70

As we end this section looking at evangelism at home and abroad, have faith that God can and will use you to reach out to others.

Paul threw Christians into prison to start with, but God turned him around to be a fearless missionary. We can never say: 'I'm not good enough to be doing mission' – look at Paul.

Look out for ways to join a team going out to spread the good news of Jesus. Ask people in your church and youth group about opportunities, look on websites (www.yfc.co.uk has opportunities for mission) and pray for guidance.

Keep going when it's difficult and leave the results to God. Paul realised that everything that had happened to him (including imprisonment) had helped to spread the good news. His amazing example gave other Christians courage to speak out too. Others may follow you when you step out for God.

When God speaks to you about mission, be glad! This is a very exciting part of your journey with Jesus and is one way of making sure you don't go to heaven without taking others with you.

CHALLENGE

Make a decision to take a new step in mission over the next 12 months. This can be at home or abroad. There is a world of opportunity – so go for it in Jesus' name.

"'In your great pride you claim, 'I am a god! I sit on a divine throne in the heart of the sea.' But you are only a man and not a god ...'"

KEY VERSE 28:2

POLITICS

WEEKEND 6/7 JUL

71

LET'S TAKE A LOOK at the big picture of our world. Politics is a part of the 'World System'. Human activity in the realms of power (politics) and wealth (economics) uses the natural resources of the planet (ecological assets), along with human resources and creativity (cultural assets), to give shape and direction to a functioning society, including technology, artistic endeavour and trade.

In prehistoric times, when communication was limited, communities were purely local in scale. But even in the ancient times of Ezekiel (597 to 571 BC, some 2,600 years ago), there was extensive international travel and trade. Today we live in a world of global connectivity. When we eat food, buy goods, dispose of waste, it always involves some other part of the planet. We are all connected.

CONTINUED ▸▸

But the problem is, the World System doesn't work for everyone. A few people may benefit from it and thrive. But sadly most others suffer and struggle to survive. For those of us who are fortunate enough, we could ignore the problem, enjoying our consumer lifestyles. But this can't last forever, as we'll run out of some things that we rely upon. Instead, we can try to get things back in balance. Development and aid charities help a lot of people like this. Thank God that they do such good work! But it still doesn't solve the underlying problem, the flaws in a global political and economic system built on human values and principles, without reference to God. In Ezekiel, God judges the empire of Tyre for such arrogance.

PRAY

In today's world, we need God's help as much as at any time in human history. Pray for insight that you will see the world (the bad and the good things) from God's perspective.

KEY VERSE v11

'The people of Edom have sinned again and again, and I will not let them go unpunished! ... In their rage, they ... were unrelenting in their anger.'

Ethnic cleansing and torture, human rights abuses and international treaty violations: these are often headlines in the news today. During the time of Amos (probably just before 760 BC in the reign of Jeroboam the second), many nations around Israel – political and military powers of the day – were guilty of abuses of human rights. Amos the prophet points out where the leaders of these nations are going wrong: in these verses there is ruthless ethnic cleansing, and the violation of the terms of a treaty, to which Tyre and Edom were party.

We live in a world where nations are interconnected with shared cultures and commerce and communications. Institutions such as the United Nations and the International Criminal Court provide us some measure of protection against governments abusing their powers or violating treaties. Not that this works perfectly – it is not 'global government' with absolute power. It only works by consensus, an agreement among the member nations. So we still hear of torture and human rights abuses, even today. For sure, it is not a new phenomenon.

MON 8 JUL

73

PRAY

God is grieved at all abuses of human rights and exploitation. Think of three places in the world where people are denied their human dignity by an oppressive government.* Pray for their protection today.

*If you're short of ideas, check out a news website like www.bbc.co.uk for more info.

'[Israel] trample helpless people in the dust and shove the oppressed out of the way.'

KEY VERSE
v7

TUES 9 JUL

74

CHALLENGE

'They sell the innocent for silver, and the needy for a pair of sandals' (v.6). This could easily describe sweatshop labour making fashionable trainers. Ask God to show you where your consumer lifestyle products may be made in exploitative ways.*

When the people of Israel hear Amos' condemnation of the terrible atrocities of the surrounding nations, they can only agree with him. 'How terrible,' they say in effect, 'such evil, such abuses.' But then Amos turns his judgment on Israel. It is easy to point the finger at other rulers and denounce them as corrupt and despotic. But Amos makes it clear that no nation is 'squeaky clean'. Even Israel's own leaders have abused their power, and God will judge them for it.

What are some of the issues identified here? See if you can spot them in the verses. You should find the following: there is economic exploitation, resulting in abject poverty for many. Also the justice system is perverted, siding with those in power against the oppressed. And where there is such corruption in leadership, there is also moral decline in the nation.

The same is true for our own nations. In the UK for example, while politicians may condemn the human rights abuses of other governments, even a quick look at history and the practices of some major companies will tell you that Britain does not have a clean record.

*www.ethicalconsumer.org might help with this.

KEY VERSE v18

'The Spirit of the LORD is upon me, for he has anointed me to bring Good News to the poor.'

Are you any good at giving speeches? The film *The King's Speech* shows a monarch with a terrible speech impediment, yet he has to learn to speak in public! To some it comes naturally and we remember their words; for example, Martin Luther King's 'I have a dream' speech, or Churchill's 'I have nothing to offer but blood, toil, tears, and sweat' – though he wasn't the first person to say those words!

In today's reading Jesus is speaking. People marvelled at Jesus' authority because unlike the religious leaders, He was not just offering empty words. Whenever Jesus spoke there was a clear demonstration of God's power to change people's lives. Jesus' 'humanifesto' in these verses is based on the prophet Isaiah (see Isa. 61:1–2; 42:7; 49:8–9; 58:6–7). Jesus understands that 'preaching good news to the poor' is not simply a religious act, but a political act too!

People in the synagogue are happy when Jesus quotes their favourite prophet. But things quickly turn nasty when Jesus tells them God's not interested in their nationalistic agenda, but cares about people in other nations, even their enemies.

WED 10 JUL

75

THINK

Jesus refuses the devil's temptation to seize control of the world's empires (Matt. 4:8–11). He also rejects an ungodly chance to make a big political show, preferring to work with people personally, even if that doesn't bring glory. What can we learn from His attitude?

'Outwardly you look like righteous people, but inwardly your hearts are filled with hypocrisy and lawlessness.'

KEY VERSE
v28

THINK

Do you think it is OK to directly challenge those in authority when they are not doing the right thing? Even if it causes offence? Jesus is not afraid to confront leaders.

In first-century Palestine, the religious leaders of the day were frustrated because the land was under the occupying power of Rome, which had political control through military rule. However, the religious leaders were allowed limited freedom to impose the Jewish law on the Jews in the local population.

For the most part Jesus got on with His work of helping people and teaching them about the kingdom of God, which means 'God's way of doing things'. However, in the eyes of the law of His day this was actually quite subversive. It was a serious threat to the religious leaders, because they thought that they were the only people who could speak on God's behalf, not some wandering preacher. And it was also a serious threat to the political authorities, because they thought anyone who could attract a crowd of several thousand people (and talk about a new kingdom) was stirring up rebellion. (And there had already been a few of those!)

While Jesus mostly avoided them, inevitably He had some confrontations with this religious elite, and usually He was not very polite towards them! Here, again, He challenges them for their double standards.

KEY VERSE v11

'Then Jesus said, "You would have no power over me at all unless it were given to you from above."'

Eventually the religious leaders decide they've had enough of Jesus, so they arrest Him, hold a mock trial, and then hand Him over to Pilate, the Roman governor. So Jesus finds Himself face to face with the most powerful political leader in the land.

However, Jesus knows that ultimately all authority comes from God, and can be either used as God intends, or abused for personal gain or political favour. So He doesn't try to defend Himself before Pilate, or plead to be set free. (Pilate has no evidence against Him anyway!) Instead, in a few words, He reminds Pilate to be cautious about 'playing God' with the power given to him. This upsets Pilate's conscience, as actually he feels powerless in the face of an angry crowd whipped up by the religious leaders. After all, if the city or nation descends into riots it is Pilate who will lose his job!

FRI 12 JUL

77

THINK

Looking again at the dialogue between Pilate and Jesus, then at Pilate and the crowd, how would you describe Pilate? Is he a strong character or a weak one? Is he a person of courage or a coward?

KEY VERSE
v1

'Everyone must submit to governing authorities. For all authority comes from God, and those in positions of authority have been placed there by God.'

Democracy is a Greek word – 'government of the people, for the people, by the people' – which can actually take many forms. Democracy is not, from a biblical perspective, necessarily better than other political systems. In fact there are no democracies in the Bible! For the Jewish people a theocracy – 'rule by God' – is seen as an ideal, but actually not attainable in a sinful world. Too often God gets replaced by some religious power structure, which is not always good.

So when Paul says here that rulers hold no terror for those who do right, we must remember that he did not enjoy the privileges of a democracy. Paul was living under the relative stability of the 'Pax Romana'

– the order that Rome imposed by its military rule. Nonetheless, this imperial power was quite brutal in conquest, and suppressed any rebellion. You couldn't vote the Emperor out! Perhaps, if Paul had been around when the empire finally collapsed (four centuries later), he might have had other advice to give!

Humans have tried many systems of government. But although all authority comes from God, whatever is done without acknowledgement of God's sovereign authority, and without reference to God's principles for good governance, will ultimately fail. This is true irrespective of how secure or stable a particular system appears to be at any given point in history. All human empires fall!

WEEKEND 13/14 JUL

79

PRAY

Pray for wise and godly governments for countries all over the world: not necessarily for democracy but for acknowledgment of God's authority.

'For you are free, yet you are God's slaves, so don't use your freedom as an excuse to do evil.'

KEY VERSE v16

Citizenship education today may not often use the word 'submit'. We don't like the idea of being submissive. However Peter teaches that one way we honour God is by being subject to the governing authorities.

This means keeping the law, even if we don't like it! It includes not breaking the speed limit, not taking things from a shop without paying for them (or buying something from a friend if we know it's stolen), not graffiti tagging on someone's wall and not making an illegal copy of that software, or film, or music track.

In the UK riots of 2011, some people with no prior criminal record began looting and vandalising, just because they thought they could get away with it. To earn the rights of citizens we must behave like citizens; not just when the eyes of the police or CCTV are on us, but at all times.

CHALLENGE

Do you follow the law of the land completely? Most of the time? Or only when you can't get away with breaking it? Does your attitude towards the law need to change?

'But Peter and the apostles replied, "We must obey God rather than any human authority."'

Now we see yesterday's lesson in practice. Peter has told us how to be a good citizen, so how come he ends up in jail? (OK, so an angel releases him before he can be brought to trial, but he'd managed to get arrested and imprisoned in the first place!) Surely, if he was doing the right thing there would be no reason at all to find himself in trouble with the law!

But then, if you look through human history, many Christians around the world have found themselves in jail for telling others about their faith, or even owning a Bible, or praying.

So is Peter failing to practise what he preaches? No, this is not the case. He is still subject to the laws of the land, but as he says, where there is any conflict with what God wants he has to obey God first and foremost. However, like a good citizen he still faces the consequences (going to jail).

Nowadays we may not be persecuted like some Christians in past centuries or elsewhere in the world, but we do often hear of religious intolerance. In recent years people have been sacked from their jobs for wearing a cross, or for offering to pray for a client.

TUES 16 JUL

81

CHALLENGE

Do you wear a religious symbol? Are you open about your faith in daily life? Be prepared to defend what you believe when challenged, but take care not to intentionally give offence.

'It is wrong to show favoritism when passing judgment.'

KEY VERSE v23

PRAY

Today, pray for people in your nation whose job it is to enforce the law and ensure justice is done. This includes the police, magistrates, judges and other court officials. Pray they would always uphold the law with integrity.

Imagine being imprisoned for a crime you didn't commit. In one case in the UK, a person was jailed for 27 years for murder, though evidence later emerged to show he was innocent! Even when a wrongly convicted person is eventually set free, no amount of compensation can give back the days of their life that have been lost. Sometimes stories like this hit the news headlines, but thankfully such miscarriages of justice are rare.

The justice system is there to ensure that the law is upheld and people's rights are defended. However, a dishonest juror can try to convict the innocent or let the guilty go free, or corrupt police may tamper with evidence. Worse than this, an unethical judge may be swayed by a personal bias, a bribe or political pressure. Such actions undermine the whole legal system. It may lead some people to think, 'I'll never get justice in the courts, so I'll take the law into my own hands, and seek revenge.'

These verses in Proverbs warn those with political or legal powers to act justly in all cases. (See also Prov. 17:23; 18:5.)

KEY VERSE v8

'Speak up for those who cannot speak for themselves; ensure justice for those being crushed.'

What advice would you give to a powerful political ruler? Think about it for a moment!

Lemuel was king of the city of Massa north east of Dumah in Arabia sometime around 1000 BC. He is given four short notes of advice by his mother. Can you spot what they are? Apart from the usual maternal cautions (don't go wild with women, and don't get drunk), there are two principles to guide his rule. These are: speak up for the oppressed, and seek justice for the poor. In other words, people who were vulnerable, disempowered, homeless and destitute were to be a priority.

Why on earth did Solomon write these down? Well, what Lemuel's mother told her son was wise advice for creating a healthy, functional society in a city state on the Arabian peninsula in 1000 BC. Solomon took it as wise advice for creating a healthy, functional society in the increasingly urbanised nation that he ruled over around 950 BC. Political leaders today could also take it as wise advice for creating a healthy, functional society in the increasingly globalised world of the third millennium in which we now live.

'Speak up for those who cannot speak for themselves; ensure justice for those being crushed.' How could we put this advice into practice ourselves?

THINK

'For Christ must reign until he humbles all his enemies beneath his feet.'

KEY VERSE
v25

FRI 19 JUL

84

Can you imagine a world where there is no legal system and no institutions of government? A world without politics? Picture it for a moment. It would be utter anarchy – everyone a law unto themselves! Unless, perhaps, everyone had all their needs met, all their rights respected, and was totally fulfilled in serving the community with all their abilities and skills. In that case, nobody would have need of power over others.

One day, at the end of all things, all human systems of dominion and authority will be done away with. This means no more oppressive abuses of power, no more unfair distribution of resources, no more exploitation of planet and people. It also means there will be a world where nobody is hungry or ill, where there is no pollution, no war, and where all wrongs are put right.

Ultimately, all rebellion against God is destroyed, and death (which is the consequence of rebellion), will cease to have any power. God's final rule is good and for the benefit of all.

According to Paul, this is the true power of the resurrection. Not just a personalised rescue plan, but the full restoration of broken human relationships and communities, so that they reflect the glory of our God.

PRAY

Keep in mind Paul's beautiful picture of God's plan for the world. Thank God for this and pray that His kingdom will come on earth.

'For the word of God is alive and powerful. It is sharper than the sharpest two-edged sword ...'

ETHICS 2
+INTEGRITY

WEEKEND 20/21 JUL

85

APPARENTLY A MAN was once arrested in the United States for stealing a book entitled *Resolving Ethical Issues*. He then tried to sell the book on. It seems that in the meantime he did not take the time to read the book!

The challenge for Christians is to be shaped by the words we read in the Bible. It is one thing to read and even admire the words in the Bible, but to allow them to shape us is different. Think of a lump of clay in a pottery studio. It needs to be moulded by the potter in order to be changed.

The Word of God is not designed or intended to just stay in the pages of a book. As today's key verse says, 'the word of God is alive and powerful.' God's Word

CONTINUED ▶

should shape us and change us. How often do you read the Bible and then almost instantly forget what you have read? Do you think about it, chew it over and allow it to penetrate into your being and mould who you are?

In this second part of our study on Ethics and Integrity we will look at how the Bible says we should approach different areas of life such as work, relationships and money. How can we live out these areas of our lives with integrity? We will go on to think about how we can interpret the Bible and its commandments for ethical living.

PRAY

Father God, thank You that you give us Your Word to help shape us. We pray that we will be renewed and shaped by what we read today. Over the next two weeks, help us to understand more about how You want us to live our lives with integrity. Amen.

KEY VERSE
v12

'We command such people and urge them ... to settle down and work to earn their own living.'

As a teenager I worked on a Saturday in a newsagent. It was hard. I had to be at work for 5:15am, so it meant getting up at 4:30am – not the kind of thing I really enjoy! Work is a big part of our lives. Statistics tell us that the average person will work 90,000 hours before he or she retires. That's 45 years of 40-hour weeks. And that doesn't include voluntary work at the church or chores around the house. Work is a huge part of our lives.

What does the Bible teach about work? What does it mean to see my own work in the same way God views it? In today's reading Paul highlights that work is a way in which we earn a living to provide for ourselves. He even goes so far as to say that 'Those unwilling to work will not get to eat' (2 Thess. 3:10). Work is not an optional extra in our daily lives.

Whatever we do, we should aim to work hard and provide for ourselves. Integrity includes working hard, rather than slacking off.

THINK

Why do you think Jesus spent His whole adult life working, until He started His ministry at 30? Why is this important?

'Work willingly at whatever you do, as though you were working for the Lord rather than for people.'

KEY VERSE v23

THINK

Who are you answerable to for your work? Perhaps it's a boss or a tutor or teacher? What would it mean for you to work for them as if you were doing it for God?

A man once came across workers cutting stones from a quarry. He asked them what they were doing. One replied: 'I am cutting stones.' The second said: 'I am earning money.' The third answered: 'I am building a cathedral.'

Joseph in the Old Testament (you can find his story in Gen. 37; 39–45) was a man who saw beyond the immediate. He faced many obstacles and disappointments in his work, not least being thrown into jail after being accused of assaulting his boss's wife, but he did not lose his belief that God had work for him to do. He also worked hard, whatever circumstances he found himself in. In terms of the way in which he conducted himself about his work, Joseph sets a great example. When we, like Joseph, see our work as part of God's plan and purpose for us, we are motivated to work our hardest and experience more personal satisfaction in our work.

We're obviously not slaves, but a hard worker is good news to an employer and to their colleagues. That's why Paul instructed the Early Church about the importance of work relationships in today's Bible reading. I encourage you to see your work as a way of serving God.

KEY VERSE
v21

'Go and sell all your possessions and give the money to the poor, and you will have treasure in heaven.'

If you looked yourself up on the Global Rich List, I think you'd be surprised. Sure you're probably not up there with Bill Gates or some of the other billionaires. But the chances are that if you live in a house made of bricks and you keep your food in a fridge and your money in a bank account, you are richer than the vast majority of people in the world.

Here in the UK we are so focused on money and the stuff we can buy with it. Even though consumerism delivers only a temporary buzz and we know it won't make any long-term difference to our lives, it's so easy to get sucked in to that way of thinking.

In Mark 10 a rich young man asks Jesus what he must do to get eternal life. Jesus' response challenges him and us. The man cared more about his wealth than Jesus or the poor, which meant that he wasn't able to follow Jesus, and he missed out on the greatest treasure of them all. How do we compare? Do we allow possessions to get in the way of our relationship with Jesus? How would we respond if we were called to give up all we had?

WED 24 JUL

89

CHALLENGE

Look at some ways you could help people who are living in poverty. Perhaps team up with some friends to sponsor a child's education or provide a village in another country with clean water, through a charity.

'If you are kind only to your friends, how are you different from anyone else? Even pagans do that.'

KEY VERSE v47

THURS 25 JUL

30

PRAY

Father, I find it easy to love those who are nice to me. But you expect more than this from me. Help me to love those who are not so easy to love, especially those who cause me pain and hurt. Amen.

Often doing the right thing and being a nice person is not actually that difficult. We can become confident that we are good people because we are generally lovely to those around us. But today's passage is quite a challenge. Just loving those who love us and being 'nice' to our friends does not set us apart in the way that God wants us to be distinctive. Anyone can be a good person if that is all it involves.

What God calls us to do is far more remarkable and makes us truly distinctive. We are called to love those who hate us and persecute us. This is incredibly difficult to put into practice and flies in the face of our natural instincts when we're hurt or offended. When someone has been killed and we see their family on the news, they often call for justice to be done and, as you would expect, feel a great deal of hatred for the murderer. But occasionally you come across someone who is able to speak of forgiving the criminal who has caused them so much hurt and pain. What an extraordinary thing to do. What can we do to stand out from the crowd like that?

KEY VERSE v24

'No one can serve two masters ... You cannot serve both God and money.'

It might just be me, but when I read about people who have big wins on the lottery I imagine what I would do with even just a bit of that money. I start to dream of the nice car and house, the holidays my family could have, the fantastic bike I'd own. At times like that there is a sense that money can buy our happiness. But all the research, as well as experience, shows that's just not true.

In the Sermon on the Mount we're reminded that if money becomes our focus then God can't be our ultimate focus: it is either one or the other. It might not be money that you are driven by, but it could be success at school or other people's affirmation. Whatever it is, as soon as that stops us from focusing on God it is a problem.

The challenge is to keep things in perspective. Money in itself isn't wrong, but the love of money is. It isn't wrong to be successful, but if that consumes you then it isn't helpful. The problem is that it's so easy to fall into the love of money, and so difficult to tell when it has happened! Regularly giving money away helps to ensure that God is your primary focus.

FRI 26 JUL

91

THINK

Spend some time honestly reflecting on what is your first love: is it God, or has something else taken over? Talk frankly with some friends about how you live your life and what you could do to ensure that God is your priority.

KEY VERSE
v20

'... your children will ask you, "What is the meaning of these laws ... that the LORD our God has commanded us to obey?"'

Why do we have rules to live by? To some people, rules are just there to be broken. For me, the most frustrating rules are those that seem to be pointless. My secondary school had a rule that our school skirts had to be below the knee but no more than two inches below the knee. To us, this seemed a completely ridiculous rule. Perhaps you remember as a child being told not to do something and when you asked why you couldn't do it, you were told, 'Because I said so!' How infuriating! After I'd heard that from my parents a few times, I vowed never to say the same thing to my own children!

Have the Ten Commandments ever struck you as a load of boring, irrelevant, out-of-date rules? They might seem this way at first glance, but the truth is far richer and more compelling. The Jewish people were told to obey these rules and teach them to their children. But in telling these commandments to their children, they would have been careful to share the story of the God who gave those rules. These commandments don't come from some kind of heavenly dictator who's detached from us and wants to spoil our fun. They come from a God who loves His people and wants to protect and bless them. If we obey God's commandments, 'he can continue to bless us and preserve our lives' (Deut 6:24). These commandments are not pointless rules with no purpose: they form a framework, a structure which will help us to live a full life in the way God intended.

THINK

How do you decide which rules are worth sticking to in the way you live your life? How willing are you to follow God's commandments?

'The Pharisees asked Jesus, "Does the law permit a person to work by healing on the Sabbath?"'

KEY VERSE V10

MON 29 JUL

94

CHALLENGE

Do you sometimes stick to the rules blindly? Might God be calling you to do something different, which goes above and beyond this?

As we mentioned yesterday, following God's commandments is really important. But living ethically is about more than just slavishly sticking to a set of rules. If it wasn't, then the Pharisees were people of real integrity! But we've already seen how Jesus called them hypocrites (Matt. 23:23) and pointed to the importance of justice, mercy and faith behind the law.

When I was at school, some of the pupils used to deliver harvest boxes to the elderly. One year, one of the pupils was delivering boxes and the lady she was meant to be visiting was not in. A neighbour agreed to look after the box until the lady returned. Whilst taking the box, she complained that nobody had ever brought her a harvest box. The girl, thinking quickly, said, 'But this other one here is for you!' Perhaps she could have got into trouble as she hadn't been told to give a box to this particular person. But the way she acted went beyond the specific instructions to follow the principle of kindness behind the whole exercise.

Jesus shows us that blindly following the rules does not always mean that we are doing the right thing. We need to allow God to use us in ways that might surprise us.

KEY VERSE
v25

'Jesus also did many other things. If they were all written down ... the whole world could not contain the books ...'

When I was little I used to get annoyed when my parents told me what to do. I longed to be older so that I could make my own decisions. As I grew up, however, and went to my parents for advice, I found that increasingly they told me to do whatever I thought best rather than giving me the clear-cut answer I was looking for.

When we are in a dilemma we may turn to the Bible for answers, and that's a really important thing to do. But we will sometimes find that the Bible does not give us the clear-cut answer we are hoping for. As today's key verse says, not everything that Jesus said or did has been written down for us. Similarly, although Jesus experienced every emotion we'll ever have to handle, there are some issues we'll face which are unique to the time we're living in.

When I make decisions, I know that my thinking has been shaped by the influence my parents have had on my life, even though they are not directly telling me what to do. In the same way, we need to get to know Jesus and His way of thinking so that He can influence the decisions we make even when the right path may not be clearly spelt out in the Bible.

TUES 30 JUL

95

PRAY

Father God, help me to turn to You for guidance when I need it. Help me to be shaped and influenced by You so that I can follow the paths You want me to follow. Amen.

'By chance a priest came along. But ... he crossed to the other side of the road and passed him by.'

KEY VERSE v31

THINK

Are you facing a difficult choice at the moment? Take a step back from it and look at what's really important in this situation.

Have you ever found yourself in a situation where you're not sure how God would want you to act? Ethical decisions are often not easy to make. The story of the Good Samaritan is a good example of how ethical decisions do not always seem entirely straightforward. To us it seems obvious that all those who walked past the injured man should have stopped to help him. However, the two men who walked past would have believed that they had good reasons for walking on by. If the man had been dead, then to have touched him would have made them ceremonially unclean. This 'uncleanness' would have lasted for a week and would therefore have been quite a major inconvenience for those whose job it was to work in the Temple, as in this story.

But just a little thought and common sense would have shown the two men what was really important in this situation! God has given us the Bible and the Holy Spirit to guide us, but He's also put brains in our heads. A little common sense can sometimes bring insight to what may seem a tricky ethical dilemma.

KEY VERSE
v19

'Understand this, my dear brothers and sisters: You must all be quick to listen, slow to speak, and slow to get angry.'

Should a pregnant woman be allowed to have an abortion? Sometimes, but not always? And if it's OK, how late on in the pregnancy should it be allowed? Should a convicted violent criminal spend the rest of his life in prison? Or should he be executed? Is it right for committed Christians to fight in a war? Does it make a difference if that war is directly defending their country? There are many ethical questions which are very complicated and very emotive. It's all too easy to get into very heated discussions on these issues.

James reminds us to listen and not get angry when we talk with others. This applies in areas of ethical debate as well. While we should stick to what we believe is right, based on prayerfully thinking about the issue in question, we should show other people that we value and respect them by listening to what they have to say, even if we disagree with them. Doing what we believe is right is important. But living out a Christian life with integrity should be more about 'caring for orphans and widows' (v.27) than getting angry in arguments.

THURS 1 AUG

97

THINK

What ethical issues are most likely to come up in discussion with your friends? What do you think is the right stance for a Christian to take on this issue? How can you ensure that you value the individuals in the discussion?

'Since we are living by the Spirit, let us follow the Spirit's leading in every part of our lives.'

KEY VERSE v25

PRAY

To follow the Spirit's leading, we first need to be filled with the Spirit! Pray now, asking the Holy Spirit to fill you, make you more like Jesus and guide you in every ethical decision you make.

Last week, I climbed a mountain with my three-year-old son. Not a real mountain, obviously. We kitted ourselves out in mountaineering gear and climbed an imaginary mountain in our house. As all good explorers do, we made sure we had a map and compass with us. As we climbed, we regularly checked our bearings on the compass. Unfortunately, the map was of no real use. It depicted Snowdonia extremely accurately, but had nothing to say about how to find our way around our house!

As we navigate our way through life's ethical maze, we have the Holy Spirit to guide us. The Holy Spirit is no map; limited to certain places, times and issues. He is a compass, able to guide us, whatever we're going through. Even when life is complex and confusing, the Holy Spirit 'will guide you into all truth' (John 16:13). So we need to spend time asking God for wisdom in the difficult ethical judgments we need to make and listening to His voice, ultimately following the Spirit's leading.

'A fool is quick-tempered, but a wise person stays calm when insulted.'

KEY VERSE V16

EMOTIONS

WEEKEND 3/4 AUG

99

EVER SAID SOMETHING in the heat of the moment and regretted it later? If you're anything like me, you'll have done that many times! One particular occasion sticks in my memory. I was helping to lead an all-night 'lock in' event with my church youth group. There was one particular boy in the group who often wound me up and on this night, he seemed even more obnoxious than usual. After hours of him finding ever more inventive ways of injuring and insulting me, I finally snapped and swore at him. He left me alone for the rest of the night, but before he went home, he told me he'd been winding me up to see how real my faith was. He reasoned that if knowing Jesus made any kind of difference to me, I wouldn't shout and swear at him, however much he provoked me.

CONTINUED »

I'm not sure about that guy's logic, but it brought home to me how important it is that we handle our emotions well. Managing our emotions badly – particularly anger – may mean other people think less of us, and can potentially do lasting damage to our relationships with them. It could even give a misleading idea of what Jesus is like, especially if we're the only Christian the other person knows.

Although I was gutted that my words to this boy showed Christianity in a poor light, I know that God forgave me. Maybe in a flash of anger you've done something that hasn't matched up with your faith. God is able to forgive you and still reveal Himself to the other people involved.

THINK

How well do you manage your emotions, anger in particular? How do your emotions affect the people around you and what impression do others get about Jesus from your behaviour?

KEY VERSE v26

'Don't let the sun go down while you are still angry ...'

This is one of those pieces of advice that everyone gives you when you get married! When I was engaged, I lost count of the number of times I heard it. But I can tell you now, everyone told me this because it's wise and important advice. In fact, it's wise advice for any kind of relationship, not just a marriage. However gracious and easy-going we might be, there will be times when we get angry with other people. It's important to admit that, because pretending we're not angry can only make the situation worse!

If you're angry and you don't express it in some way, the sense of anger and frustration builds up and festers, making the issue far bigger than it really needed to be and creating resentment between you and the other person. I find I just can't sleep if I'm angry with someone, especially my wife. It's far better to talk things through with the other person involved as soon as you can than to put it off and hope it will just go away. As Paul points out, if we don't deal with our anger, it gives the devil a foothold in our lives (v.27) and allows him to damage our relationships with others.

MON 5 AUG

101

PRAY

Lord Jesus, please help me to handle my anger wisely. When I'm angry, help me to talk things through with the other person, even if that's really hard. Please make me kind, compassionate and forgiving. Amen.

'A gentle answer deflects anger, but harsh words make tempers flare.'

KEY VERSE v1

TUES 6 AUG

102

CHALLENGE

The next time someone is winding you up, pause before you answer. Decide to defuse the situation, rather than saying something harsh and making it all worse.

It was the final of the 2006 football World Cup. The captain of the French team, Zinedine Zidane, was playing in his last ever international match and got into an off-the-ball tussle with Italian defender, Marco Materazzi. The details of what happened next are hazy, but people say the chain of events went something like this: Materazzi pulled Zidane's shirt. Zidane remarked to Materazzi that if he wanted to swap shirts, he'd have to wait until the end of the game. Materazzi responded by saying something extremely rude about Zidane's mother. Zidane lost his temper and head-butted Materazzi in the chest. However much the referee saw of what happened before, he certainly saw the head-butt, and he sent Zidane off in his last ever international game.

I suspect that Materazzi was going out of his way to make Zidane angry, but in any case, this is a striking example of how our words can affect a tense situation. When tempers are rising, if we pause for a moment and give a gentle and gracious answer, it can go a long way to calming people down. If we speak out of anger and say something harsh or insulting, it can make things ten times worse.

KEY VERSE v34

'Then Jacob tore his clothes and dressed himself in burlap. He mourned deeply for his son for a long time.'

A couple of years ago, a good friend of mine lost his dad. It was all very sudden and even now, no one's really sure if it was suicide or just a tragic accident. My friend found it incredibly hard to come to terms with his dad's death. We all supported him as well as we could and tried to help him work through his grief. But we just had to accept that this would be a process: it was going to take time. Even now, my friend gets very upset around the time of year when his dad died. It's understandable, of course. When you're that close to someone, having that person taken away from you is always going to be hard to take.

Jacob goes through similar feelings in today's reading. In this case, it's a little different, because Joseph isn't actually dead, but Jacob has no way of knowing that at this point and acts as if he were. His family do their best to support Jacob in his grief, but there's a limit to what they can do. Grief takes time. If we or someone we know is grieving, it's important that we understand that and *allow* it to take time.

PRAY

Pray for anyone you know who is grieving. Ask God to comfort them, heal them, help them express their grief and come to terms with it in time.

WED 7 AUG

103

'When Hezekiah heard this, he turned his face to the wall and prayed to the LORD ...'

KEY VERSE v2

THINK

God is with you, however dark life may look. How will that affect your attitude to grief and suffering? How will it affect the way you pray?

When I moved away from home and started university, I had to leave a lot of good friends behind. This was really hard to do and in fact was a kind of grieving process. Obviously, it's nowhere near as bad as someone dying, but it is true that there is an element of grief involved in leaving people or a place we love. It was a huge comfort to me to know that God was in this situation. I believed this was the right step for me to take and that however hard it was, God would be with me and also with the friends I was leaving behind.

I don't know if Hezekiah was quite as confident as I was that God was with him, and the circumstances he was facing were far worse than mine. But in his darkest moments, Hezekiah calls out to God and finds He is there and is involved. As Hezekiah relies on God to hear him and help him, God steps in and does just that. When we're grieving, God is with us. We might not see the kind of miraculous healing that Hezekiah saw, but even in our darkest moments, God is there with us. Grief really is hard to deal with and it can take time, as we saw yesterday. But however long it takes, God is with us to comfort us, guide us and give us His peace.

**KEY VERSE
v25**

'Worry weighs a person down; an encouraging word cheers a person up.'

I'm a bit of a worrier. Actually, that's an understatement. I'm 'a lot' of a worrier. And when I'm worried about something I have to do at work, home or even at church, I often get quite grumpy and distracted and have trouble sleeping. At times like these, I really appreciate the support my family give me. They don't have to do anything that special. Just a bit of encouragement works wonders. And maybe a slice of cake too ...

These verses from Proverbs point out a simple but vital truth. Our words have tremendous power to build other people up. Worry and anxiety can really weigh people down and make them feel depressed and alone. Just a quick encouraging comment can make a world of difference to them. We might not realise at the time that what we've said has helped someone, but if we get into the habit of encouraging others, we may be pleasantly surprised by the number of people who come to us and tell us we made a difference to them.

CHALLENGE

Choose to be an encourager. Whenever you meet someone this week who seems worried or anxious, make a point of saying something encouraging to them.

KEY VERSE v13

'No one said a word to Job, for they saw that his suffering was too great for words.'

At times of national mourning, people will often observe a minute's silence. On Remembrance Day in the UK, for example, everyone stops what they're doing and is completely silent, to remember the sacrifice made by people who've died, fighting in the cause of freedom. At times like these, there's an acknowledgement that sometimes grief, pain and suffering are too great for words. Only silence is fitting.

In this passage, Job has lost everything. His home, his property and family have all been wiped out. He's now going through intense physical pain, too. Job's suffering has affected him so severely that his friends can hardly recognise him (v.12). They want to help Job and comfort him, but realise that no words they could say would really do justice to the level of his pain. All they can do is sit with him in silence.

When someone we know is suffering, encouraging words can often make a difference. (See yesterday's reading.) But at other times, especially when they're in a lot of pain, we don't need to say anything at all. It can even be glib and patronising if we do say something. Just being there is often enough. With the Holy Spirit in us, we can carry the presence of God with us and have His wisdom to know what to say and do as we try to comfort our friends who are suffering.

PRAY

Think of someone you know who is really suffering at the moment. Pray for that person and ask God to let you carry His presence with you when you spend time with them.

"'Everything is meaningless,' says the Teacher, 'completely meaningless!'"

KEY VERSE v2

MON 12 AUG

108

Ecclesiastes can be a difficult book to read. A lot of it seems so bleak and hopeless. It was written by King Solomon, who had everything a man could possibly want and yet, so much of the book expresses his disillusionment and depression. Today's key verse is a prime example. Despite everything he's seen, done, owned and experienced, Solomon concludes that everything is meaningless.

But Ecclesiastes gives us an insight into what life can sometimes be like. Life will sometimes seem bleak and hopeless, maybe even meaningless. No matter how much we own, how much we've experienced or however many people love us, all of us will feel down occasionally. For some of us, this can go as far as clinical depression. But getting depressed doesn't make someone weak or a bad Christian.* Sometimes, life just takes us through the valley of the shadow of death. But God is with us, even then (Psa. 23:4). And if we continue to trust Him, we will eventually find, as Solomon did, that there is a meaning and purpose to life after all: to know God and follow His plan for our lives (Eccl. 12:13).

*If you're struggling with depression, don't suffer in silence. Talk to a friend or your youth or church leader. You might also benefit from some counselling. www.acc-uk.org could be a good place to start.

PRAY

Thank God for being with you, even in your darkest times. If you know someone who's struggling with depression, pray that they will discover the same meaning and purpose that Solomon did.

READING: 2 Corinthians 1:3-11

KEY VERSE
v8

'We were crushed and overwhelmed beyond our ability to endure, and we thought we would never live through it.'

Paul is one of the greatest Christian leaders who ever lived. So how come he starts this letter sounding so depressed? It's worth looking at some of the incredible pressure he was under. Later on in the same letter, Paul explains that he had been imprisoned, whipped, beaten, stoned, shipwrecked, isolated, persecuted, hungry, thirsty and in constant danger (2 Cor. 11:23–27). Under these circumstances, he can be forgiven for feeling a little down!

It's also true that we're not immune to depression just because of our status within the church. If even Paul struggled in this area, we might too. A pastor I know, who is an amazing leader and preacher, is very open about the fact that he has struggled for years with a very severe case of obsessive compulsive disorder.

Paul's response to feeling 'crushed and overwhelmed' is crucial. It would have been understandable if he'd descended into self-pity and given up. But in verses 9–10, he goes on to explain that these unbearable pressures forced him and his companions to rely on God and that God carried them through it all. Because of this, Paul can praise God even in the direst of circumstances (vv.3–4).

TUES 13 AUG

109

CHALLENGE

Choose to rely on God today, even if you're feeling 'crushed and overwhelmed'. He is the God of all comfort, who comforts us in all our troubles' (vv.3–4, NIV).

'Here on earth you will have many trials and sorrows. But take heart, because I have overcome the world.'

KEY VERSE v33

110

PRAY

Are you facing challenges now? Ask the Holy Spirit to help you overcome these things.

After my son was born, I found it very difficult to cope. My whole thought process had to change, so that I always thought about the baby first, rather than myself or even my wife. The constant sleep deprivation didn't help, I was under pressure at work at the same time and my wife was also exhausted and quite ill, so needed a lot of support. It all combined to leave me feeling very low and highly stressed. For a while it seemed hard to see any kind of end to it all. But, slowly, things began to change. My son started growing and getting more independent. The pressure lifted at work. My wife started feeling better and I began to feel I could handle it all.

The disciples know Jesus is about to leave them. They must be wondering how they will cope with the dangers facing them. Jesus doesn't pretend that these challenges will disappear. In fact, He says the opposite; that they will have 'many trials and sorrows'. But He reassures them that He has overcome the world. Because of this, through the Holy Spirit, they can overcome the challenges they face. We will all face times when we feel we can't cope. But these challenges won't last forever. And the Holy Spirit can help us overcome them.

KEY VERSE v4

'Always be full of joy in the Lord. I say it again – rejoice!'

Let's make this absolutely clear: God never promises to make us happy. Fulfilled, yes (John 10:10). Wise, yes (James 1:5). He promises never to leave us (Heb. 13:5) and He promises us hope and a future (Jer. 29:11). But 'happy'? No, sorry, I can't find that in the Bible anywhere. You could even argue that the opposite is true!

Paul had a nice, comfortable life before he met Jesus. But after Jesus called him and Paul began to serve him, things started getting an awful lot harder!

And yet, Paul's letters are brimming over with joy. Despite the rejection, hunger, loneliness and physical beatings he suffered, despite the fact that he had to write a good number of his letters in a prison cell, his writing is full of praise, gratitude and joy. I don't believe Paul was happy. But Paul seems to be suggesting that we can *choose* to be joyful, even if we're not happy. Whatever we're going through, God is still God. He still deserves to be worshipped for who He is and praised for the good things He's given us, even when life is hard. If we choose to do that, it does make a difference. We can have the same sense of joy and gratitude which Paul had and be inspired to keep going.

THURS 15 AUG

111

THINK

What can you praise God for today? Even if life is hard at the moment, think of the good things He has given you and choose to thank Him for them.

'Surely your goodness and unfailing love will pursue me all the days of my life, and I will live in the house of the LORD forever.'

KEY VERSE v6

I suggested yesterday that God never promises to make us happy. Sorry if that came as a bit of a disappointment. There's one exception to this. Our destiny is heaven, where there will be no more pain or death or suffering (Rev. 21:3–4). Then, we will be utterly satisfied and peaceful and, yes, happy in God's presence. David echoes this idea in Psalm 23. He comforts himself by remembering that he 'will live in the house of the LORD forever'.

But there's more. David doesn't pretend that life will always be easy in the meantime, but he realises that God will be with him in all of the trials he faces. In fact, he seems to believe that the times when life seems hardest will be the times when God blesses him and provides for him most powerfully. David mentions God's rod and staff (v.4) which represent guidance and protection, but within the context of walking through the darkest valley. God provides for him and blesses him lavishly (v.5), but this happens in the presence of his enemies. Happiness is waiting for us in eternity. But in the meantime, let's keep our eyes open to how God is blessing us, providing for us and protecting us now – even in the hardest of times.

FRI 16 AUG

112

PRAY

Ask God to remind you of specific lessons from this series of readings. Ask Him to show you how He is with you now, blessing you and providing for you.

'Seek the Kingdom of God above all else, and live righteously, and he will give you everything you need.'

MISSION
+ EVANGELISM

AS WE TAKE A THIRD look at Mission and Evangelism, we'll hear about how God challenges young people to go and do something for Him. This may mean stepping out of comfort zones and could include travelling; or it may involve doing something within our communities. The challenge is to do something!

So, what holds us back? What gets in the way of us stepping out for God?

We can create barriers for ourselves: we may think that we are not confident enough or that God couldn't use us. There may even be some practical or financial barriers, like those Sarah faced: not only did she have to raise finance for her mission trip and get her passport

CONTINUED ▶▶

in time but she also had to overcome her fear of flying for the first time.

Whatever barriers are stopping you, try to look at them positively and pray for God's help in each situation. Here's what Sarah thought about her mission ...

'Going to Antigua was amazing and challenging. I would recommend doing a summer mission to anyone, n ot only to meet great people but to learn more about yourself and God. I've learnt to rely on God more now that I'm back. However many barriers you need to break, trust God it is worth it.'

How will you respond to this challenge? What is God calling you to do? Pray about any barriers you will need to overcome to follow God's calling.

PRAY

Father, show me what You're calling me to do and where You want me to go. Help me to see past the barriers that stand in my way and to trust in You for all things. Give me a heart for others – to see them come to know You. Let me take up the amazing challenge You have ready for me. Amen.

'The Kingdom of God is near! Repent of your sins and believe the Good News!'

Jesus wants each of us to hear His good news. Our reading today is set at the beginning of His ministry: Jesus tells people that the kingdom of God is near – that the rule of God is about to be lived out and shown to everyone by Him. Then He tells them to repent.

Right now stop and think about the rule of God. Do you need to turn your life around to face the way of Jesus again? Stop. Think. And turn your heart and life again towards God.

Next Jesus walks past some fishermen and tells them to follow Him. They instantly drop what they are doing and do as He says. Now what is fascinating about this situation is that Jesus is a rabbi, and when rabbis picked their disciples to follow them they picked the best of the best students around. The fact that these guys were fishermen means that they had left school early; they were the least likely to be picked to follow a rabbi. So when Jesus called them, it was just like you receiving a phone call from the Prime Minister or England Football Manager who signs you up for the cabinet or the first team!

Jesus picks ordinary people to do extraordinary things.

MON 19 AUG

115

CHALLENGE

Repenting is changing the way we think and act to God's way of thinking and acting. It's something we should do regularly. Make it a habit to stop, rethink and turn again. Take time to put things right with God today.

'How terrible for me if I didn't preach the Good News!'

KEY VERSE
v16

CHALLENGE

How desperate are you for your friends to become Christians? Pray and ask God that He would increase the passion in your heart for them to know Him.

When I was ten, I was at a friend's house playing a Game Boy for the first time. For those of you born after 1990, a Game Boy was the greatest invention of its time – like a Nintendo DS but black and white and about four times the weight and size! As soon as I held it in my hands and heard the music I had to have one. Every time I went round to my friend's house to get my fix, it just made it worse. My life became one big mission to get a Game Boy.

Paul is a man on a mission. Look at the passage. He says he has no choice (v.17), compelled by God to tell other people about Him (v.16). He is a desperate man.

When we think about the things we crave and have a desire for in our lives, do we have that same desperation and mission to tell others about God? As Christians, our hearts should be passionate to see our friends come to know Jesus – just as we have other passions in life!

Why? Because Jesus has shown a love to us that is so massive we should be desperate to share it. And, just as my mission to get a Game Boy grew the more I touched it, the greater our heart for our friend should become the more we get to know God and His love.

READING: Philippians 2:5–11

KEY VERSE v5

'You must have the same attitude that Christ Jesus had.'

Josie came from Brazil to work with Norwich Youth for Christ for a year. She was involved in every area of their work including schools, gospel choirs, regular youth events, youth clubs and special events. Josie constantly looked for ways to serve and never complained about any of the things she was given to do, no matter how exciting or not!

Her team leader, Mark, said: 'Throughout all these activities we have seen Josie displaying a godly character and love for people. As the time for her to leave has come closer, young people have been saying how much they will miss her, and it's obvious that her genuine love for them has made a very positive impact.'

How we act and the things we do can really impact the people around us. This can be a negative impact or, like Josie's, a really positive impact. The great thing about Josie is that she is able to show others that her faith in God makes a difference in her life. The young people of Norwich were sad to see her leave – but what she has done will stay with them for a long time.

THINK

What impact do you have on those around you? How do you show people that you are a Christian?

'Live clean, innocent lives as children of God, shining like bright lights …'

KEY VERSE v15

THINK

What are the major pressures on you at the moment? What can you do to change your situation? How can you shine brighter as a star?

I was talking to a woman recently about evangelism and she told me that, because of the way she lives and acts, her friends call her 'the shiny person'. Isn't that amazing? And it's just what Paul is talking about. He tells us to shine like bright lights by leading clean, innocent lives in a world full of crooked people.

The life God calls us to lead is distinctively different from the way that the rest of the world lives. Young people are placed under immense pressure to act and behave in certain ways that are in deep contrast to the way Jesus teaches us to live. As we come under these pressures, are we blending into the dreariness or are we shining like stars? As our friends are getting drunk, smoking, sleeping with their partners and gossiping, are our lives distinctively different?

What is amazing is that when you live in a godly way it challenges people and they ask questions, giving you an opportunity to share your story. I remember the first conversation with my best mate about God; he couldn't believe that I wouldn't have sex before marriage. Seven years later, through how I stuck by what I said and the way I lived my life, he became a Christian.

KEY VERSE v8

'Then I heard the Lord asking, "Whom should I send ...?" I said, "Here I am. Send me."'

What's the best gift anyone has ever given you? For me, it was the bike my wife gave me last Christmas – absolutely brilliant and just what I needed! But have you ever thought about which gifts God has given you?

God has given Lizzie a gift and a passion for working with young people. It's a real calling on her life. Lizzie responded to this calling and used her gift to serve God this summer. Here's what Lizzie says:

'I heard about an opportunity to go to South Africa during a gap year with Youth for Christ called yfcone. I really felt I wanted to experience youth work in a different culture and wanted to use my passion to serve God in South Africa. I felt a real peace about going and God provided everything I needed in an amazing way. The trip was indescribable. I learnt so much about the South African culture, about God and about myself. I saw God touch so many lives, by using me out of my comfort zone. Some of the things I saw and experienced will stay with me forever.'

Imagine if Lizzie hadn't responded to her calling to use her gift for God. What an experience she would have missed out on.

FRI 23 AUG

119

THINK

What are your gifts? How does God want you to use those gifts? How could you serve Him with them?

KEY VERSE v11

'... they bowed down and worshiped him. Then they opened their treasure chests and gave him gifts of gold, frankincense, and myrrh.'

My son loves drawing. He'll draw with anything that comes to hand. If there's no paper available, he'll even draw on the walls! For my last birthday, he gave me a card he'd made himself with a drawing in it. Unfortunately, he's only three, so he's not exactly a skilled artist! I needed a little prompting to realise he'd drawn a shark for me! But I really didn't care about that. I knew he'd done his best and given me something he'd put time and effort into.

Yesterday, we mentioned the gifts that God gives us and how we can use them. But it's also worth thinking about what gifts we can give to God. The Wise Men were among the first people ever to meet Jesus and meeting

Him definitely had a cost attached for them. They undertook a long and potentially dangerous journey to see the newborn King and as they worshipped Him, they gave Him rare and expensive gifts. They clearly realised that Jesus deserved the best of everything they had to offer: their possessions, their time, their energy and their worship.

Jesus deserves the best of everything we have, too. Let's commit our time, energy and resources to Him by serving Him and taking His good news to others. Of course, in the end, everything we have comes from God anyway. So even giving Him the best of what we have is only offering Him a part of what was His to start with!

PRAY

Lord Jesus, I worship You. You are awesome and You deserve everything I have. Please teach me to give You the best of myself by serving You and other people. Amen.

'For a child is born to us, a son is given to us ... And he will be called: Wonderful Counselor ... Prince of Peace.'

KEY VERSE v6

MON 26 AUG

Ever received a gift that was not quite to your taste or even downright weird? My mum recently gave me an apron for my birthday. Nothing wrong with that in itself, but I'm not much of a cook, and even when I do cook, I never use an apron! (Then again, perhaps my mum was dropping a hint that I should help out more around the house!) Whatever Mum's reasons were for giving me the apron, I've never used it. It just sits in a drawer in the kitchen.

Jesus came into this world so that we could be saved from our sin. He gave Himself up as a sacrifice for the cost of our sin, in order that we could have a relationship with God. Today, remember this gift of salvation that was given to us freely – but cost Jesus dearly.

This gift is for sharing. We should not put it on a shelf to gather dust, or hide it in a drawer, like I did with my apron. We should take the gift of salvation through Jesus to every place and every person we can.

CHALLENGE

What will you do with the gift of salvation that comes through Jesus? To which people and places will you take this gift?

'The Spirit of the LORD is upon me, for he has anointed me to bring Good News to the poor.'

This passage shows Jesus setting out what He came to earth to do. He shares this news with the people in the synagogue in Nazareth. The first thing we notice is that Jesus says that the Spirit of the Lord is upon Him. We must also remember that when we share our faith, our power comes from the Holy Spirit. So, just like Jesus, we need to keep asking to be filled with His Spirit.

Jesus asked us to make disciples just as He did, so our mission is to continue the work He started. Jesus preached good news to those who really needed to hear it. So let's not forget to tell those around us – and to bring good news every single day.

There's much in life that holds people back, preventing them from being the people God wants them to be. This might be addictions, jealousy, gossiping etc – and making other things priorities before God. We are called, like Jesus, to help people to be set free from this negative stuff – for Jesus tells us to release the prisoners.

TUES 27 AUG

123

CHALLENGE

Think about the many ways Jesus took good news to those around Him. How can you imitate Him in the way you speak and act? Don't forget: Jesus didn't just tell it, He also lived it. He always practised what He preached.

'... people ... brought sick family members to Jesus. No matter what their diseases ... the touch of his hand healed every one.'

KEY VERSE v40

124

THINK

Who do you know who is oppressed or needs healing? How can you bring Jesus' actions and words to them today?

Yesterday we looked at what Jesus told people about His ministry and what He was sent to do. In today's reading, Jesus shows us two further ways in which He was good news to those around Him.

First, Jesus promises to release the oppressed. In the first story He comes into contact with a man tormented by an evil spirit. Jesus releases the man from the evil spirit and he is set free.

Do we know people who are oppressed? Is it those being bullied? Or perhaps people living in poverty? It's amazing how many people find faith as a result of Christians who are prepared to support them in their time of need.

Secondly, when Jesus sent His disciples out, He didn't just send them to preach at people, He sent them to heal those who were ill. We carry this very mission in our lives. God does heal today, both physically and emotionally. He longs for us to take this gift to our friends. God can heal people through us: what a way to prove to people that He exists and can be good news for them!

'He will wipe every tear from their eyes, and there will be no more death or sorrow or crying or pain.'

When I was a kid, I thought heaven was going to be a beautiful, massive field, with an amazing play area, where it was always sunny! Or maybe you thought it was going to be a swimming pool full of chocolate! What do you think about heaven?

I am not the judge of who goes to heaven, that's God's job. But the Bible is very clear that heaven exists and those who follow Jesus will live with Him there forever. If you had a pile of tickets to a free party, would you keep them to yourself or would you invite as many people as you possibly could?

In today's passage, John gives us a picture of what heaven is going to be like. No more death, sorrow, crying or pain – and life forever with God. That's something that I want to look forward to and really want my friends to be invited to. One of the biggest reasons that we tell our friends about Jesus is because heaven and hell are real places. And the only sure way of going to heaven is by making a decision to make Jesus King of our lives.

THURS 29 AUG

125

PRAY

Dear God, thank You so much for preparing heaven for us and for sending Jesus to enable us to go there. I am so grateful. Please help my friends to understand heaven, and help me to have the courage to invite them along. Amen.

'He jumped up, stood on his feet, and began to walk! Then ... praising God, he went into the Temple with them.'

KEY VERSE v8

FRI 30 AUG

126

Can you remember how it felt when you first became a Christian? I don't know about you but I just wanted to tell everyone. I was also so grateful to the people who had introduced me to Jesus.

Charlotte had been in the youth group for ages but she had never quite understood what Jesus had done for her and how much He loved her. Her friends kept talking to her, then one evening someone told her about the hope she could have in Jesus. That night Charlotte joyfully told the person who had introduced her to Jesus just how grateful she was, and how happy God had made her.

In this passage, Peter and John give a man an experience of Jesus – and much more than he expected. His gratitude to them must have been huge. When we introduce people to Jesus they will have the same gratitude, no matter how long it takes or how many prayers or setbacks we may face on the way.

Let's keep going, keep praying and keep showing and telling those around us about Jesus. One day they may feel the same gratitude as Charlotte and this guy – whose lives were totally transformed. And we will be blessed through our prayers being answered.

THINK

Who introduced you to Jesus and has helped you in your walk with Him? Why not drop these people a text to thank them for the investment they have made in you. Then pass on this investment – share what you have been given!